The Last Bookseller

THE
LAST
BOOKSELLER

A Life in
the Rare Book Trade

GARY GOODMAN

University of Minnesota Press
Minneapolis · London

Published by the University of Minnesota Press
111 Third Avenue South, Suite 290
Minneapolis, MN 55401-2520
http://www.upress.umn.edu

ISBN 978-1-5179-1257-4 (hc)
ISBN 978-1-5179-1661-9 (pb)

A Cataloging-in-Publication record for this book is available from the Library of Congress.

Printed in the United States of America on acid-free paper

The University of Minnesota is an equal-opportunity educator and employer.

30 29 28 27 26 25 24 23   10 9 8 7 6 5 4 3 2 1

For my best partners

My dear wife, Mary Pat, and our six children

Meghan, Ben, Nolan, Jonathan, Colin, and Steven

Contents

Introduction ix

1. Four Thousand Bad Books *1*

2. Book Scouts and Dead Booksellers *12*

3. Billions of Books *23*

4. All for the Want of a Book *29*

5. A Book Fair with the General *41*

6. Bookman's Alley and McCosh's Mansion *52*

7. Beating the Bushes *60*

8. A Bookstore in Stillwater *66*

9. Hoarding and Horse Barns *80*

10. Travels to Book Towns *91*

11. The King of Hay-on-Wye *101*

12. The Mormon and the Map Thief *109*

13. North America's First Book Town *121*

14. The Book Collectors *133*

15. The *Stillwater Booktown Times* *139*

16. The Beginning of the End *143*

17. Survival Tactics *153*

Epilogue *165*

Appendix: Travel Journal *169*

Acknowledgments *177*

Bibliography *179*

Introduction

As long past as 1930, I had a hunch that
the talkies would make even the best selling
novelist as archaic as silent pictures.
F. SCOTT FITZGERALD, *The Crack Up*

OKAY, so I know I'm not the last bookseller. People still sell books. But I'm one of the last of a certain *kind* of bookseller. The kind that for six hundred years rooted around basements, book bins, and bookstores looking for, sometimes, rare books or, more often, secondhand books.[1] They were the hunter-gatherers of the book business, the travelers and pickers, who spent their lives saving books that might otherwise have been lost. They are, now, nearly extinct, driven to ground by the machines—the cell phones, personal computers, and, especially, the internet—that replaced them at the end of the twentieth century.

The Last Bookseller describes my career as a used and rare book dealer before and during this seismic shift. It is, on one level, a conventional memoir: how I started as a bookseller in 1982; the remarkable, larger-than-life, and sometimes criminal people I met buying and selling books; the unusual books I found and the weird places I found them. But on another level, it is a picture of—and a tribute to—those traveling booksellers who, beginning with the invention of the printing press in

---

[1] "Secondhand," "used," "rare," and, less often, the fancier "antiquarian" are used interchangeably here. They all refer to previously owned books and so are, in essence, the same thing. Some books just cost more than others.

1440, rescued and preserved so many of the rare books and significant manuscripts that survive today.

Most booksellers' memoirs are about finding a pamphlet by Edgar Allan Poe at the bottom of a coal chute and selling it for a half a million dollars.[2] Not this one. I stumbled into the book business when I walked into a small used bookstore in East St. Paul, Minnesota, and, despite not knowing a thing about books or business, bought the place. Later, with a couple of partners, I opened another store in the small tourist town of Stillwater, Minnesota, which became so successful and caused so many other booksellers to move there that it became known as a "book town." Book towns—that's right, towns full of books—were an actual thing during the roaring '90s of the secondhand book trade.

Richard Booth, the self-proclaimed king of Hay-on-Wye, Wales, and the originator of the official Book Town movement, comes to Stillwater in this story, as does Larry McMurtry, the famous author and secondhand bookseller who created a book town in his hometown of Archer City, Texas. Melvin McCosh, the Minnesota bookseller who sold books from his run-down mansion on Lake Minnetonka, makes an appearance, and so does A. S. W. Rosenbach, the flamboyant rare book dealer who, in the 1930s, bought original manuscripts of books like *Ulysses* and *The Canterbury Tales*. Oh, and then there's the book scout who took showers in public restrooms using tubes and garbage bags.

The rare book business in the 1980s and 1990s was also marked by an unusual level of thievery, forgery, and treachery, so several criminals turn up here, including Stephen Blumberg,

[2] Travis McDade writes in *Thieves of Book Row,* "A remarkable number of the memoirs of booksellers are basically anecdote delivery devices . . . rich with stories of acquisitions and near misses . . . This is true of most of these types of books simply because that is what people want to read."

the St. Paul native who was the most prolific book thief in history; John Jenkins, the Texas bookseller and world-class poker player who killed himself (or was murdered) while standing in the middle of the Colorado River; and Mark Hofmann, the Mormon rare book dealer and forger who blew up two people with pipe bombs to cover up his crimes.

When the internet came along it was, for secondhand booksellers, like a lawyer waking up and discovering that all his clients had gotten law degrees. Before 2000, it took years of experience to become a successful secondhand bookseller. After 2000, anyone in their pajamas with a box of books, a cup of coffee, and a cable connection could buy and sell books online. Between 1990 and 2000 there were nearly four hundred used and rare bookshops in New York City; now, there are fewer than seventy. There were almost fifty in Minneapolis–St. Paul; now, fewer than ten. The internet wiped out many secondhand booksellers—and their traditional bookshops—almost overnight.

So the kind of bookseller I'm talking about here is a vanishing breed.[3] Before the last dog dies, I wanted to describe what it was like to make a living in this curious and unconventional business. I traveled enough—throughout the United States, the United Kingdom, and Canada—and saw enough to know my experiences reflect the changes that occurred in bookselling at the end of the twentieth century and the beginning of the twenty-first. These stories are told from my perspective but are meant to give a realistic picture of this age-old occupation. The booksellers I describe here might not be the last ones, but they are likely the last of their kind.

---

[3] Distinct from independent booksellers, who sell new books and whose bookstores are the last line of defense against the internet juggernaut. Their stores are also under siege, but so far the internet hasn't figured out how to replace them.

1. Four Thousand Bad Books

In the middle of my life,
I found myself in a dark wood,
for the straight way was lost.
      DANTE, *The Divine Comedy*

O N A MARCH MORNING in 1982 I walked into F. Fithian, Books,[1] a small secondhand bookstore on Arcade Street in East St. Paul, Minnesota. The name was above the front door in crooked wooden letters, and in the window a handmade sign announced that the store was going out of business. The place wasn't much bigger than a rich person's walk-in closet. I had never been in a used bookstore before in my life and was struck by the musty smell and the chaos, confined, as it was, to such a small space.

The walls were lined with cheap particleboard bookcases. There were toppled stacks of books on the floor, and more books—novels from the turn of the last century, self-help books, beat-up paperbacks—spilled from broken boxes. Prominently displayed, face out, on plastic stands were a few newer children's books. Sections in the store were marked by paper scraps thumbtacked to the shelves, the subjects written in thin ballpoint pen. The fiction section was full, with books stacked from floor to ceiling, but other sections had only five or ten books, with signs like "Italian Renaissance" or "Eastern Philosophy" tacked below them. Beyond the cases, behind a

---

[1] A few names have been changed to protect the innocent.

counter made of plywood and two-by-fours, sat a small man whose name, I learned, was Frank.

Frank was a stocky man in his grayish fifties who wore a rumpled suit and smelled like he'd had a few Bloody Marys for breakfast. He told me he was closing the store because of, as he called it, his "bad ticker"—heart troubles had forced him to retire as a newspaper reporter, and now angina or heart palpitations or A-fib had foiled him again.[2] "It was always my dream to own a nice bookstore," he said, gesturing around, "but this was all I could afford." He wanted to sell the business but couldn't, "because people around here don't appreciate books."

The store itself was in a small pocket of down-market businesses in a working-class neighborhood at the intersection of Arcade Street and Maryland Avenue. The cars that drove by were usually on their way somewhere else. On Frank's side of Arcade there was a drugstore, an empty hair salon, and an antique shop. Kitty-corner, on Maryland, was a liquor store with bars on the door and a yellow sign in the window that advertised quart bottles of Ripple wine for ninety-eight cents each.

I was thirty-one years old then and lived three blocks away in a rented duplex on Wheelock Parkway with my wife, Mary Pat, and our two children. I earned what could be charitably called a living working the night shift on a hospital unit that treated violent and mentally ill adolescents. In fact, a few days before my visit to Frank's store, some of the little rascals had planned to take over the unit by killing the male counselor— that would be me—by hitting him over the head with a sock filled with metal belt buckles. An alert nurse discovered the plot

---

[2] I later came to doubt the heart story. I saw Frank a few years later in downtown St. Paul, and he looked as healthy as a horse.

and called the police, but the incident reaffirmed my belief that working with people who wanted to kill you was not a viable long-term profession.

So the thought of buying a going concern, filled with valuable books—I liked books, didn't I?—from a man who, but for a heart condition, would not be selling this plum in the middle of East St. Paul made perfect sense. "If you sold the business instead of closing it, how much would it be?" I asked Frank, just out of curiosity. Frank's eyes lit up at this prospect. "Let's see," he said, climbing up on the chair behind the counter and grabbing a pencil. "You have your books—four thousand good books, handpicked. Then your fixtures—the bookcases, display racks, etc. Then there's the goodwill, the name, the location . . . I'd probably sell the whole thing for $25,000."

Twenty-five thousand! I could barely pay my rent, much less $25,000. I already worked double shifts on the psychiatric unit two or three times a week. The car I drove, a 1969 Volvo I'd bought for $200, didn't have working windshield wipers. On cold nights I had to bring the battery into the house so the car would start in the morning.

Frank saw the shock the figure generated. "Of course," he continued, "I have the heart condition. Plus, I'd have to move all the books that don't sell, so I'd probably take $10,000."

I turned away. I didn't have $10,000 either. But Frank continued to negotiate with himself. "Then there's the lease on the store," he said, "which runs another three months. I'll be on the hook for that. So, I'm thinking . . . I'd hate to do it, but I'd take $2,000 for the whole thing." He paused. No reaction from me. "On a contract for deed at $100 a month." I perked up. "And nothing down," he added.

And that's how I became the owner of a used bookstore in East St. Paul.

---

jacket. Covers worn, hinges broken, pages yellowed. $2.00. Postage $1.25." The ad for *The Adventures of Pinocchio* did not specify a date or publisher, so the bookseller looking for it was going to get quotes for hundreds of copies, most of them better than Frank's. I glanced through the other postcards and noticed the going rate for most of his books was two dollars.

Frank also suggested that I could put in a popcorn maker and sell ten-cent bags of popcorn to elementary students on their way home from school. If I sold 1,800 bags a month—or 60 bags a day, including Sundays—I could just about cover my rent. Then he produced the contract for deed, collected his first hundred dollars, and handed me the keys.

"Good luck," he said, and walked out the door.

When the consequences of what I had done became clear, I thought that if selling a secondhand bookstore to someone who didn't know the first thing about used books was a felony—and it should be—Frank would have gone to prison.

The store on Arcade Street was a dismal hole. So much so that during the eight years I was there, every other event in my life— from the kids learning to ride a bike to tomatoes ripening on the vine—was thoroughly documented with photos, but when I looked for a picture of the store to include here, I couldn't find even one, so I went to East St. Paul and took a picture of what it looks like today. It was empty but, ironically, in its last incarnation, had been a cell phone and computer repair services store.

Mary Pat's father, a successful businessman, was horrified when he saw the place. It convinced him, finally, that his only daughter had married an idiot, a conclusion that Mary Pat's six brothers, who were all on solid career paths, had reached long before. Only my childhood friend Mark Ziegler—who had endorsed, it must be said, many other bad decisions—was

The old Arcade Street store in 2020.

supportive. Otherwise, the skepticism from my friends and family was universal.

During my first week I tried to make sense of what I had gotten into. The overflowing fiction section was packed with old novels: *A Cigarette-Maker's Romance* by F. Marion Crawford; *The Magnificent Ambersons* by Booth Tarkington; *The Last Days of Pompeii* by Edward Bulwer-Lytton. There were shelves of Reader's Digest Condensed Books, piles of paperbacks priced at $1.25 each, and book club editions of popular novels by James Michener, Ken Follett, and Judith Krantz. Now that I knew where Frank got the books, I could see why they had been rejected by every book freak in town. The store was not a gold mine but a strip-mined pit.

Since I didn't know anything about the book business, I thought I should get some advice, some tips on how to move forward, maybe even make a connection with the wider Twin Cities book world, so I called Larry Dingman—a prominent Minneapolis dealer who specialized in modern first editions— and asked him to come over. When he got to the store, Larry methodically went through the shelves. After about ten minutes he turned to me and said, "This is the worst, most picked-over stock of books I've ever seen." And no wonder, I thought, since they were the leftovers Frank had rescued from every down-market book sale in town. Larry did give me some advice: (1) I should get rid of all the books I had; (2) I should get better books (he did not elaborate on what kinds of books those might be); and (3) "Don't hire anyone to work for you. It'd be a waste of money."

And, like Frank before him, Larry walked out the door.

I had three customers and sold thirty-six dollars' worth of books that first week. Never mind that I worked the night shift at the hospital from midnight until eight in the morning, went home, ate breakfast, and was back at the store from ten until five. I learned that Frank's "winter is slow" comment really meant that you could have murdered someone on the corner of Arcade and Maryland and no one would have noticed. Not, certainly, the geriatric customers going into Roy and Greta's drugstore on the corner. Every so often one of the more muddled would wander off and walk by my store, but none of them ever came in, which I would have appreciated, if only to have someone to talk to.

I'd go to my bookstore hellhole every day and sort through the paperbacks, book club editions, ex–library books, and other rubbish Frank had sold me. As I looked over this empire of bad books, one that was of some consolation was a beat-up copy of *Books and Bidders* by A. S. W. Rosenbach, a bookseller from Philadelphia who made a fortune selling rare books to the libraries created in the 1920s and 1930s by wealthy robber barons and industrialists like Andrew Carnegie and J. P. Morgan. If nothing else, Rosenbach's story showed me that people could actually make a living selling used books.

Rosenbach describes how as a young boy he hung around his uncle Moses Polock's bookstore in Philadelphia, a store founded in 1780, just before the end of the American Revolution.[3] When Polock bought it in 1831, he became the first bookseller in the United States to specialize in rare Americana. He acquired, among other things, books from George Washington's Mount Vernon library and a batch of letters from English and American statesmen addressed to John Hancock, a signer of the Declaration of Independence.

As Rosenbach remembered in *Books and Bidders*: "First as a publishing house and bookstore combined, Uncle Moses's shop became a meeting place for publishers and writers. Here it was that the ill-fed [Edgar Allan] Poe came in 1835 to talk modestly of his hopes and dreams. Such men as James Fenimore Cooper, William Cullen Bryant, Noah Webster, and Herman Melville might be seen going up or coming down the narrow staircase leading to the second floor."

At that time and, indeed, throughout history, secondhand bookstores have been gathering places for writers, politicians, poets, and revolutionaries. James Joyce, Ernest Hemingway, and F. Scott Fitzgerald hung out at Sylvia Beach's Shakespeare and Company in Paris. City Lights in San Francisco was a center for counterculture politics in the '50s and '60s.

---

[3] Henry Knox, George Washington's secretary of war, sold both new and secondhand books. He learned what little he knew about military strategy and tactics at the start of the Revolutionary War from books. The nation's repository for gold bullion, Fort Knox, is named after him.

And in the 1960s Melvin McCosh's bookstore in Minneapolis had Bob Dylan and other local radicals as customers and conversationalists.

Rosenbach recalled a conversation his uncle had with a customer about Edgar Allan Poe: " 'Of course Edgar was a genius, in spite of being a gambler and a drunkard—in spite of it, I tell you!' The other, a thin man of lesser years, his long, inquiring face meditative in the twilight, said, 'You are right,' he agreed. 'But what difference did it make? Would 'The Raven' have been any greater without his gambling and drinking? I doubt it.' "

A. S. W. earned a doctorate from the University of Pennsylvania in 1901 with a dissertation titled *The Influence of Spanish Literature in the Elizabethan and Stuart Drama.* Financial troubles and his parents' ill health forced him to leave school and form the Rosenbach Book Company in 1903 with his older brother Philip: "I felt a renegade. I had deserted the halls of learning for the bookshop; I had given up my fellowship to enter a business that would, perhaps, put money in my purse. I did not, when at college, appreciate what a high adventure the business was to prove, the excitement and anxiety of the chase, and that I had a better chance, a far greater opportunity, to unearth unpublished documents, and uncover original source-material, than ever I could have as an instructor in English in some university."

Rosenbach went on to buy and sell some of the most significant original manuscripts in the English-speaking world, including part of Chaucer's *Canterbury Tales,* Lewis Carroll's *Alice's Adventures under Ground,* and James Joyce's handwritten *Ulysses.* He loved books and reveled in the attention he got when these purchases made headlines. He almost single-handedly put together the rare book collections of the Widener, J. P. Morgan, Folger, Huntington, Houghton, and Rosenwald libraries.

According to biographer Richard Ellmann, Joyce was in-
censed when he heard Rosenbach bought the *Ulysses* manuscript in 1924 in Paris at auction for the bargain-basement
price of $1,975 and memorialized his discontent in a poem:
"Rosy Brook he bought a book / Though he didn't know how
to spell it / Such is the lure of literature / To the lad who can
buy and sell it."

Books weren't Rosenbach's only passion. "For him . . .
drinking was a daily occurrence," notes Travis McDade in
Thieves of Book Row. "He was 'riding the crest of his wave,'
one of his biographers noted, and 'the wave had a high alco-
holic content.' He was rich, respected, and had the impulse
control of an adolescent."

My daydreams of becoming a big-time bookseller ended
when another worker walked by on the way to pick up some
kielbasa without so much as a sideways glance. I didn't know it
then, but my purchase of the store on Arcade Street had put me
on the lowest rung of the lowest ladder in the book business. I
had four thousand bad books in a bad location and not a dime
to my name.

2. Book Scouts and Dead Booksellers

Let him who is in search of
knowledge fish for it where it lurks.
MICHEL DE MONTAIGNE

I DID WHAT I COULD to attract customers: I made displays
of best sellers from the 1970s. I put the two newer children's
books—God knows where Frank got those—in the window. I
put dollar books in boxes outside the store to attract the cost-
conscious book lover, but stopped that after (1) a dog peed in
one of the boxes and (2) some elementary kids took another
box and dumped it in front of the liquor store. The liquor store
owner—who sold, remember, quarts of Ripple wine for under a
dollar—complained to Roy that the boxes in front of my store
made the neighborhood look bad.

On the days that Mary Pat worked—she taught community education classes—she took our daughter, Meghan, with
her and brought our baby son, Ben, down to the store, where
he'd sleep in a playpen in the back room. "Don't let him crawl
around in here," she'd tell me. "He'll get all dirty and probably
catch some disease."

Early on I figured that the only way I was going to survive
was by finding, as Larry put it, better books—books I could
quote to other booksellers. To find out what "better" meant,
I turned to the *AB Bookman's Weekly,* which I studied reli-
giously. By going through the long lists of books wanted and
books for sale I got a vague idea of what people were looking

for and started going to library sales, thrift shops, estate sales, other bookstores, flea markets, and abandoned storage lockers, often on my way home from working the night shift at the hospital. It was there I met the book scouts and, sometimes, downright criminals of the book-buying underworld. I was new, unfamiliar with their rituals and hierarchy, a curiosity to the other book people. "Are you the idiot who bought Frank's store in East St. Paul?" they'd ask.

Some of the most educated and honorable people I have ever met were in the book business, but some of the most unsavory and illiterate were book people too. Those who operated at my low level—and some I met as I moved up the ranks—could be strange and troubled individuals. Loners, survivalists, and petty criminals regularly bought and sold used books on the open market. The real professionals, the people who made a living at it, were the book scouts, many of whom I came to admire and respect. Anyone who could buy books and make money doing it was a wonder to me. A successful book scout needed a quick mind, an encyclopedic knowledge of books, and a thick skin.

Book scouts knew a good book—meaning a book that would sell—when they saw one and sometimes would stumble on a book, or a batch of books, that would pay for a month's worth of gas and doughnuts or a new mattress for the back of the van. They didn't need to know (or even, in most cases, care) that *Ulysses* was a literary masterpiece or anything about Plato's theory of forms; they just needed to know that the book had a market. Scouts were a primary source of new stock for the larger secondhand stores, so the stores were dependent on them. Good scouts could, and often did, threaten to take their books elsewhere if they felt they weren't getting a fair price.

Larry McMurtry started as a book scout, as did John Dunning, the author who wrote *Booked to Die, The Bookman's*

Wake, and others in a series of mysteries about a bookselling detective. Dunning eventually started Old Algonquin Books in Denver. A short story he wrote for *This Week in Denver* in 1986, called "Bookscout," gives a good picture of a book scout's day:

> He [Joel] had scouted the East side, hitting all the stores from Broadway to Peoria Street. He had turned up some nuggets; not diamonds, not even rubies, but a few good garnets. There was a first edition Nelson Algren, the best book he'd found in four months. Would that it were one of the early ones, *Never Come Morning,* say, or, please God, *Somebody in Boots.* But even *A Walk on the Wild Side* was good enough to cover expenses and pay for a few meals. It was a $50 book to collectors. Mark Ramsey, the book dealer on East Colfax, could get that for it in this condition without much trouble, and that meant at least $15 to Joel.

Once I started going to the sales, book scouts would stop by the store to sell me books or, just as likely, tell me their tales of woe. One, Andrew, described how he lived in his van and took "showers" in public restrooms using tubes and garbage bags. He wondered if he could sleep in the back room of my store when the weather turned cold because the shower idea, brilliant as it was, meant that sometimes he had to drive around soaking wet when it was twenty below. He said he could be like a night watchman and make sure no one stole any of my books. I told him the chances of my even selling a book were slim, and the chances of someone stealing one were about zero, so I declined his generous offer.

Another scout, named Gideon, was so far off the grid he lived in the woods under a tarp. "I don't like the shelters," he told me. "Too many bums." He came to book sales on a bike with a large basket on the handlebars, even in the winter. Gideon told me that when warrants for driving without a license, past-due student loans, unpaid child support, and missed court dates prevented his return to civilized society, he got into the book business. Now that he was self-employed, he didn't have to worry about interviews, suits, or background checks—a great comfort, no doubt, for someone who seemed to be a lost soul.

No discussion of book scouts would be complete without mentioning the book-theft ring engineered by some New York booksellers in the 1920s and '30s. This ring recruited students and drifters to travel across the country and steal rare books from naive and unprotected libraries. "A well-trained and experienced scout could identify fifty to one hundred books of value on a library's shelves and, after some practice, manage to steal from as many as three libraries a day," writes Travis McDade. This rampage continued for over five years, covered the entire Northeast, and resulted in the loss of millions of dollars' worth of books. It was considered the worst period for library book theft in American history. This was the sort of thing—not, by the way, confined to this one time period—that gave legitimate book scouts a bad name.

The places to buy books, the venues, so to speak, were also many and varied. Take the flea markets, those outdoor sales held in parking lots, where sellers rent spaces, put up card tables, and sell antiques, glassware, paper products, doorstops, home preserves, mittens, and, sometimes, kittens. The sellers would arrive in battered vans and broken-down cars in the early morning to set up for the day; they were often retirees, but some could be a step away from either a homeless shelter or the county workhouse. The flintier types were deeply tanned from standing in the sun all day and, in my memory, missing at least one tooth.

There was a flea market every Saturday in White Bear Lake, where spaces rented for twenty dollars. I'd pack my car the night before—a car that fit in with the rest of the beaters in the parking lot—with a folding table and several boxes of books and leave at around five a.m. to set up for the sale. Remarkably, Mary Pat liked going to these sales and sometimes would pack up the two little ones and come with me. I bought books and met some interesting people but never made much money on the flea market circuit.

On Fridays and Saturdays were the estate sales. If you think your scrapbooks, high school yearbooks, genealogy that traces your family history back to the Civil War, military medals, or wedding photos will be saved and passed down from generation to generation, think again. These are usually left in the house and are part and parcel of most estate sales. And not the best part either, since they usually don't sell and are hauled to the dump once the sale is over.

If there were books advertised at an estate sale, I'd get up at three in the morning, hope whatever hulk I was driving would start, and wait in line for a sale that started at eight. For a decent sale in a middle-class neighborhood, with antiques, furniture, perhaps a car, and books advertised, the line started to form even earlier. The first person to arrive handed out "temporary numbers," and these were exchanged for "real numbers" when the estate sale people showed up at around seven.

Imagine a Minnesota winter, with the temperature at minus twenty or so, cars lining the block, engines running, exhaust fumes rising, filled with dealers waiting for an estate sale to begin. The people who attended the estate sales—besides the general public, who were a nuisance to everyone else associated with the process—were antique dealers, furniture dealers, car dealers, coin dealers, and book dealers. Anyone who hoped to make money off the dead or dying's earthly possessions.

A guy named Karl was often the first person at these sales and would hand out the temporary numbers. After a few mornings drinking coffee and eating doughnuts with Karl—whose Christian name was originally spelled with a C, but he changed it to a K in honor of the KKK—in his van, I learned that he bought furniture at estate sales and sold it at an auction house down in Iowa. He used the proceeds to buy guns and donate to white supremacist groups. Karl owned some land in Wisconsin and had converted an old corn silo into a warehouse and living quarters. He must not have done a very good job on the silo, because after a heavy rain the roof caved in and destroyed some furniture he was going to send to auction.[1]

You wanted to get to an estate sale early so you could get into the house with the first wave of buyers. Depending on the size of the house, this could be anywhere from twenty to thirty people. If you were late and your number was, say, thirty-one, you'd stand in the cold while the people inside ransacked the house and bought everything worth buying. Book dealers and book scouts went straight for the books; they'd yank them from the shelves and throw a coat over them or stand around and yell things like "Stop it!" or "This whole shelf is mine!"

---

[1] An interesting—and somewhat related—example of the easy entrance into the book business and the fringe elements it attracted is that of Reinhold Pabel. Pabel was at a German prisoner-of-war camp in Illinois during World War II when he escaped, went to Chicago, and opened a used bookstore on the North Side. By dealing only in cash and saying that his accent was Swiss and not German, Pabel was able to run the Chicago bookstore until 1953, when he was finally tracked down by the FBI. He told his story in *Enemies Are Human*, published in 1955. After serving his time he moved back to his native Hamburg and opened two bookstores. He died in 2001 at the age of ninety-three, but one of his stores is still operating under the name of Antiquariat Reinhold Pabel.

The scene at estate sales made the basement sale at Filene's in New York look like a tea party. When they were done grabbing stuff, people in parkas—sweating, shouting, and shoving— would stumble out the front door, gasping for air.

This intensity carried over to the annual book sales held by churches, libraries, and universities. Some of these sales were huge, with ten or even twenty thousand books, and book people would line up for hours before they started. Store owners might hire someone to wait in line for them and then, right before the sale, show up and take the hired hand's place. One book scout, named Shane, who sold technical books through the mail, took offense at this practice. He said it was unfair to the "working man." Despite his socialist tendencies, Shane wanted very high prices for his technical books, and if someone asked why they were so expensive, he'd get belligerent and shout, "Show me your copy!"

At one library sale at a Catholic boys' prep school early in my career I walked in and saw two bookcases full of two or three hundred books, all in brand-new condition. A sign above the cases said the books were two dollars each. Two dollars! What were these people thinking? My budget then for a book was about fifty cents. The place was nearly empty and no one else was looking at those books, so I bought a couple—a Kurt Vonnegut and something by John Cheever—and got out of there. Too rich for my blood.

When I got back to my store, I discovered that these books were part of an exclusive club called the First Edition Circle that in the 1960s put out limited and signed books by famous living authors. Both of my books were signed and, I think, limited to 150 copies; someone had donated an entire collection of those books to that sale. It was too late to go back that day, so I went the next, but by then all the books were gone. I sold my two books to another dealer for about a hundred each—a lot of money for me in those days. To make this memory worse, I never saw another First Edition Circle book in my thirty-plus years in the book business.

A final book-buying opportunity came from dead booksellers. One morning as I was getting off the night shift, I found out that Malcolm, a bookseller with a store in downtown St. Paul, had died and his estate was selling off his books. He and Harold Lensing—who later started Harold's Books on West Seventh Street—had worked together after World War II but became bitter rivals when Malcolm inherited a bookstore that Harold felt should have gone to him. The latter started his own store in about 1948 or 1949; he first had a shop on Jackson Street and then, in 1968, started Harold's Books at 186 West Seventh Street.

I'd been to Malcolm's store once. When I went that first time he was sitting on a ledge by the front window wearing a brown overcoat and a fur hat with ear flaps, reading a newspaper. I learned later that Malcolm didn't heat the store and would only turn on the electric lights if a customer promised to buy something. I was only able to see some of his books—and those were covered with dust—because when I came out of one section empty-handed, he wouldn't turn on the lights for the next one. He was so unpleasant and his books so hard to get at I never went back. Fellow bookseller Paul Kisselburg recalls, "I remember going there several times. At first, he would not let me in until I promised to buy something. Then, he would not turn on the lights. I had to use a flashlight. I bought a few things. Then, on subsequent trips, he would let me in and turn on the lights! He warmed up to me a little bit."[2] On the morning of the

---

[2] I want to acknowledge here, as I do at the end, the contributions of my friend and fellow traveler Paul Kisselburg to this book. His ongoing comments and corrections, his knowledge of the book business, and his enthusiasm were invaluable. His observations—and my observations about him—are a big part of this story.

sale, the lights were on and the place was crawling with book-sellers and book scouts. I heard they found Malcolm, dead, by the window where I had first seen him.

On another morning I went to an auction at a storage locker in St. Paul that included the leftovers from a dead bookseller named Morris who'd had a small shop in Minneapolis. The books were mostly old language textbooks and outdated car manuals that I would not have touched in my later years, but they were cheap, so I bought a few batches. I'd never been to his store, but according to Paul, "Morris's shop was on South Ninth or Tenth Street in downtown Minneapolis. He lived there and had several rooms of books in the garden level of an old apartment building that was torn down twenty or more years ago. I bought a few books from him, but he never had anything good. [Melvin] McCosh knew him. He was mugged in downtown Minneapolis not too long before he died. I re-member the smell of his store very well. Not an unpleasant odor, just old and booky."

Malcolm and Morris, like so many marginal booksellers of this era, died alone, their last days spent with lunch cooked on a hot plate in the back room or eating a TV dinner watching the *Antiques Roadshow*. At the lower levels, secondhand book-selling was a tough, hand-to-mouth existence, and not many of these old war horses made it out of the book business alive.

At the other end of the spectrum were the great bookstores and booksellers in the Twin Cities, who I got to know out of des-peration. If I couldn't cover the checks I'd written or the bills due by the end of the month, I'd pack up boxes of books and take them around to sell to other bookstores. Getting a bank loan was out of the question—the average criminal had a better credit rating than I did—so I hawked books like this to stay afloat. The only difference between me and a book scout then was that I had a store and a permanent mailbox.

On Snelling Avenue in St. Paul, in the Midway district, there were three secondhand bookstores within a few blocks of each other—Midway Book Store, Booksellers et al., and James and Mary Laurie Booksellers—and two smaller stores close by. In the 1980s and early 1990s Midway was the center of the Twin Cities book world; Harold's Books was nearby, and Rob Rulon-Miller sold books out of his house on Summit Avenue. Tom and Kathy Stransky bought Midway Books in 1980 when it was a small paperback trading store and built it into a world-class secondhand book operation. The Stranskys were, and continue to be, more passionate about books—especially buying them—than any booksellers I've ever met.

Booksellers et al. was a cooperative store open from 1983 to 1993 started by Steve Anderson, Ruth and Ann McKee, and

Midway Book Store, St. Paul, Minnesota.

Virg Viner. Ruth, who died in 2007, was a wonderful lady and a great bookseller. She specialized in children's books and wrote *McKee's Price Guide to Children's Literature*. Steve knew the generation of older booksellers before Paul Kisselburg and I came on the scene and has been involved in just about everything related to the book business ever since. Paul says, "Steve knew everyone and remembers everything. He knew all of those very important men from the decades prior to this. Stan Nelson, who sold his store to Leland Lien; Heddan; Ross and Haines; early McCosh; and others. They were the men who created the used book business in the Twin Cities that we then broadened and enjoyed through the glory years." If anyone could write a history of bookselling in Minnesota, it'd be Steve Anderson. Steve's last physical store was in Hudson, Wisconsin; he closed it in 2007, but he still sells books through the mail.

There was another pocket of bookstores in Dinkytown, near the University of Minnesota. The aforementioned Larry Dingman had his Dinkytown Antiquarian Books there. Jim and Kristen Cummings had a store called the Book House. Biermeier's Books, owned by Bill Biermeier, was a few blocks away. In the suburbs, Dave Dale had the Bookdales in Richfield and Jean O'Donoghue had a store, called J & J O'Donoghue Books, in Anoka.

These were all superb, thriving secondhand bookstores, with stocks of sixty, eighty, or a hundred thousand books. On Saturdays, they'd be so busy you'd have to elbow your way into the cat book section. I hawked books to all of them. Now most are gone—Midway, the Lauries, and the Book House are still around but do most of their business online.

3. Billions
of Books

Economics, as always, vouchsafes
us few dramatic turning points.
JOHN KENNETH GALBRAITH

FOR A BEGINNER, as I was, learning the business was like being in a foreign country without knowing its language or customs. You had to look at masses of books, wonder if anyone wanted them, and decide what they were worth. In economic terms, this was the supply, in the first instance, the demand, in the second, and the market, in the third.

There is so much printed material—from scientists and philosophers, gossips and self-help gurus—because that is one way ideas and emotions get out into the world. Books are the physical manifestation of the human mind. They can be simple reporting or artistic fiction, scientific studies or movie-star biographies, but whatever the subject, a whole lot of books are cranked out day after day, year after year. Google Books calculated in 2010 that there had been nearly 130 million individual titles published since the invention of the printing press. Over 700,000 new titles come out every year.

Just go into a library sometime and look at the books. There are books on heart health, gardening, pets, science, relationships, celebrities, miracle cures, and mystical experiences, among a myriad of other subjects. And not just one or two, but shelf after shelf. It's amazing how many there are. According to Lewis Buzbee's *The Yellow-Lighted Bookshop,* "If you read one book a week, starting age five, and live to be eighty, you will have read a grand total of 3,900 books, a little over one-tenth of one percent of the books currently in print."

Current best sellers have print runs of 2 million or more, but assume, over time, that the average print run is 2,500 copies. That's 335 *billion* physical books published to date, only the smallest fraction of which will have any demand on the resale market. Before the internet, secondhand booksellers sorted (without a computer at their fingertips) through this immense pile of cheap paperbacks, academic treatises, popular novels, religious screeds, autobiographies, technical manuals, comics, coffee-table books, cookbooks, and bad poetry and picked out the books they could sell.

Experienced used booksellers could recognize the salable books in this pile almost instantaneously—not unlike, say, a doctor who runs through thousands of possible diseases in a matter of seconds when making a diagnosis—but the sheer volume of material they had to deal with also explains why it took so long to learn the business. As Marvin Mondlin and Roy Meador note in *Book Row,* "The typical bookman started in the profession very young, often as a book scout, worked as a bookstore employee, acquired some know-how, and finally found a modest amount of capital to launch a store of his own." While a few booksellers were genuine scholars, many of the more well known only had high school educations. They were a mile wide and an inch deep—they knew the best books in a subject without knowing much about the subject itself.

Before the internet, booksellers absolutely controlled the used and rare book market, so they could, up to a point, control prices; they were limited only by what other booksellers charged and what customers would pay. Academics and nostalgic book hunters were good customers, but book collectors were the real driving force behind the business. These sometimes odd, obsessive people collected books about almost anything: paperweights, toy soldiers, dogs, doorstops, fire engines, paint, plants, fleas, butterflies, cooking, cartoon characters, fishing lures, and even, though rarely, cats. For them, the internet has taken the fun out of searching for that rare or elusive item. The thrill of the chase, which drives collectors as much as anything else, just isn't there anymore.

Like art and antiques, the market for a book depends on how many copies are available—its supply—and how many people want it—its demand. A first printing of *Action Comics* issue #1, which was published in 1938 and features the first-ever appearance of Superman, sold for $3.2 million in 2014. The same year, a first edition of Hemingway's masterpiece *The Sun Also Rises* sold for $50,000. The Superman was sixty-four times more valuable than the Hemingway simply because more people wanted to own it. It is not rarity—with the original dust jacket, a first edition of *The Sun Also Rises* is about as scarce as a first *Action Comics*. Or literary merit—for that, you'd probably have to give the nod to Ernest Hemingway over Jerry Siegel and Joe Shuster, the creators of Superman. Or age—*The Sun Also Rises* appeared twelve years before *Superman*.

The market for a book also changes over time, sometimes due to external events. A first edition of *A Game of Thrones* by George R. R. Martin, published in 1996, sells for $750, largely due to the popular TV series. Right now, a signed first edition of Donald Trump's *The Art of the Deal* can sell for $1,000; before Trump became president, signed copies sold for $10. First editions of early Potter books by J. K. Rowling sell for many thousands, but you can buy a first edition of *Winnie-the-Pooh* by A. A. Milne, published in 1926—arguably a more significant children's book—for $300.

When books really were hard to find, before the *AB Bookman's Weekly* and the internet, the market for used and rare books was greater than it is now by an order of magnitude. As Travis McDade notes in *Thieves of Book Row,* the "antiquarian book trade now is a niche industry that caters to a very small percentage of the American buying public . . . It is difficult to overstate how large the trade in rare books was [in the 1920s and 1930s], or how many people depended on it." *Publishers Weekly* reported on rare book auctions, major acquisitions, and the health of individual secondhand bookstores. The exploits of rare book dealers were regularly covered in national newspapers. A. S. W. Rosenbach "appeared so often in the *New Yorker*'s 'The Talk of the Town' that the magazine seemed to have someone stationed in his office." The *New York Times* had regular columns on rare books and noted, on December 16, 1923, "Literary property is selling at boom prices in the markets of the world. Attics, cellars, closets, old trunks and other abandoned repositories in the Old World and the New are being rummaged for hidden literary treasures to supply the demand."

With the arrival of the internet, grandma rummaged through her attic and found rare books that suddenly weren't so rare anymore. And instead of buying a book from Molly the bookseller down the block, she could buy it online and have it delivered the next day from any Clara, Tessa, or Alexa with a cable connection. This was especially hard on midrange book dealers, who owned most of the secondhand bookstores. The demand for a good portion of the books they relied on to make a living evaporated. Before, booksellers had to know the price and market for books. Once this information was everywhere, booksellers had no competitive advantage over anyone else.

So what about starting, from scratch, a secondhand bookstore today? Say the average bookseller needs twenty thousand decent books, priced at an average of $25 each, to make a living—not far from what the usual store has in stock. To get those books, the fledgling bookseller has to either buy them online, where bargains are hard to find, or fight the wolves at book, estate, and garage sales. Even if they can get the books at a modest price, say $5 each, that's still a $100,000 investment. Never mind that buying twenty thousand books one at a time like that would take twenty years.

Then there's setting up shop: building bookcases, advertising, paying rent, and so on. Call that part of it $25,000. So, conservatively, it takes $125,000 to start a bare-bones operation in, probably, a bad part of town. If the bookseller needs $27,000 to live on—the minimum required for a single person to survive in most places—and has, say, $4,000 a month in expenses, the store needs to sell $6,300, or 250 books, a month just to make ends meet. But here, too, the bookseller is competing with the whole world. People won't spend more than $25 on a used book these days without looking it up on their phones to see if they can get it cheaper somewhere else—and they usually can. With all the aggravation and risk, and the ability to sell books online, starting a store just doesn't make sense anymore. The forces that have made finding out-of-print books more efficient and driven down prices have made stores an untenable way to sell secondhand books. The stores left are set pieces, like heritage farms or disco bars—places people visit when they want to see the way things used to be.

The truth is most of the secondhand stores still around are owned by people in their sixties or seventies who would like to get out of the business but can't. They drag themselves down to the store a few days a week to see if there's any cash in the till and only survive because most of their business, too, is done on the internet. Stores that continue beyond their first owners are either legacies—where a son or daughter takes over—or operations purchased, on very generous terms, by employees. These second-generation stores rarely last long. One guy I knew, who pinched pennies until they bled and operated a store for over thirty years, sold his business to a couple of his employees. They bought elaborate computer and phone systems, hired a bunch of people, and remodeled the front entrance of the store, all on credit. The store was gone in a year.

There is one foolproof way to get out of the book business, as illustrated by a book published in the 1930s called *The Private Papers of a Bankrupt Bookseller.* The preface is by a neighbor who found the bookseller's papers after the bookseller died. Of the bookseller, this neighbor says, "The deceased came to our town and bought a bookselling business. The business he bought was not in a good way when he bought it and he paid too much for it. He had fancy ideas as to what books he would keep and what books he would sell." Proving the neighbor's point, the bookseller writes, "I don't think I ever parted with any book from all my stock but with a feeling of regret . . . even though I must sell to live—to lose possession [of a book] wrenches at me."

To bring this discussion of the economics of the book business back to my own story, I could paraphrase Charles Dickens in *A Tale of Two Cities* and say I got into the book business at the best of times and the worst of times. It was the best of times because someone like me, who didn't know the first thing about, really, anything, could wander into a small bookstore in East St. Paul, buy it, and develop a body of knowledge that was valuable and proprietary. I could travel and buy books that I could sell for more than I paid for them and find books for people who had nowhere else to turn for that elusive copy of *Danielle and Her Chicken Farm.* I was a god among men. I was a bookseller. It was the worst of times because a few years after I got into this six-hundred-year-old business the internet began to exert its destructive—from, of course, the booksellers' standpoint—influence.

4. All for the Want of a Book

All honor to poor Don Vincente of Aragon. His
name shall always be cherished by lovers of books.
I have known men to hazard their fortunes, go on long
journeys halfway around the world, forget friendships,
even lie, cheat, and steal, all for the gain of a book.
A. S. W. ROSENBACH, *The Unpublishable Memoirs* [1]

BACK ON ARCADE STREET, Roy was worried I'd go out of business because he had a hard time renting the spaces in his building. The place next to me was empty for two years before a salon called Sassy Nails moved in. The owner, Keira, was a twentysomething brassy blonde who had taken out $30,000 in student loans for cosmetology school but could only find minimum-wage jobs, so she decided to go into business for herself. I figured she'd be there six months, tops, but it wasn't long before she had three chairs cranking out manicures and pedicures full-time.

Now people might think I have exaggerated for cheap dramatic effect how many odd and unstable characters there were in the book business. Surely most in this venerable profession

---

[1] Rosenbach might have been talking about himself. In the 1920s a book detective for the New York Public Library system said of the bookseller that he had "a rather disquieting familiarity with some of the phases of book theft's more difficult techniques and methods. Indeed, in certain circumstances it is not impossible that Rosenbach's evident acquaintance with the professional devices of the book thief . . . may lead to an inquiry in his own direction."

were honest, upstanding, and levelheaded. And that's true enough, but there were plenty who weren't.[2] Some of the most notorious criminals in history happened to be booksellers or book collectors. A. S. W. Rosenbach reminds us of the Spanish monk Don Vincente, who in the early 1800s abandoned holy orders and opened a bookshop in Barcelona with books he stole from monastery libraries. After being outbid at auction for one book he coveted, the former monk broke into the winning bidder's house, stole the book, and burned down the premises—with the bidder still in it. Don Vincente killed eight other people in book-related crimes and was executed in 1836, but not before becoming the patron saint of evil booksellers.

Even with the limited exposure I had to the business in the 1980s, I had some contact with two of the most famous book criminals in history: Stephen Blumberg and John Jenkins. Blumberg, known as the Book Bandit, was from St. Paul and was arrested in 1990 for stealing 23,600 books worth an estimated $20 million (in 2021 money). Jenkins, the self-styled Texas Bookmaker, was once president of the Antiquarian Booksellers' Association but became so enmeshed in gambling, forgeries, and loan sharking that he (allegedly) shot himself while standing in the middle of the Colorado River.

Stephen Blumberg first came into the Arcade Street store in 1989 wearing an overcoat and black woolen gloves with the fingers cut out, like a character from a Dickens novel. He was

---

[2] You don't have to look far to find them—there's a new story every week. One recent example is the autobiography *Can You Ever Forgive Me?* by Lee Israel and its film adaptation starring Melissa McCarthy. Israel was a destitute writer who forged letters from deceased authors and playwrights and sold them to New York rare book dealers. The story makes plain that the book dealers were, at the very least, complicit in allowing this fraud to continue.

seedy, with greasy hair and a big mustache. According to the wife of one of Blumberg's friends, he was so unkempt that she "felt she had to Lysol the chair he sat in whenever he stopped by." He made an impression on me because he had these big googly eyes. He came in a few times, mostly on weekends, and would stand inside the front door, looking around with his buggy eyes. If I talked to him or asked if I could help him, he'd leave. Finally, he asked if I had a rare book room; as I recall, I said that not only did I not have a rare book room, I didn't think I had any rare books. With that, he left and never came back. When I found out later who he was, I was mildly insulted that he didn't even bother looking around to see if I had any books worth stealing.

Blumberg came from a wealthy St. Paul family and lived on an annual trust fund payment of $72,000 he got from his grandparents. He was a loner who, when he walked by the Victorian houses being torn down on Summit Avenue, picked up antique doorknobs, stained-glass windows, and doorstops. To research these items, he stole reference books from the University of Minnesota. He liked the books more than the doorknobs and, over twenty years, "liberated" nineteen tons of rare books from libraries, museums, and bookstores. Unlike most book thieves, Blumberg didn't steal the books to sell but to "protect" them from their current owners. (Not selling the books was one reason he was able to operate undetected for so long.) His base of operations was a run-down seventeen-room house in Ottumwa, Iowa, where he stored, in perfect order, his stolen collection.

One store he hit heavily was Harold's Book Shop in St. Paul. He robbed the place twice, first by breaking in through the back door and then by hiding in the basement until the store closed. During the second robbery, Blumberg stripped the store of all its valuable books. This crushed the owner, Harold Lensing, and led him to sell the store to Paul Kisselburg and Ted Henry in 1986. As Paul remembers, "Harold was, indeed, devastated. He continued to run the shop for a couple of years after the second burglary, but he never fully recovered. He was mistrustful of everyone. He no longer enjoyed the business and wanted to sell out. He negotiated with a few people and eventually agreed to terms with me and Ted."

Hiding in the basement was a typical tactic for Blumberg when it came to getting into a library or bookstore after regular hours. In a January 1994 article for *Harper's Magazine,* Philip Weiss describes some of his methods:

> He would avoid alarm systems or set them off a couple of times and observe the security response. He'd squirmed through ventilation ducts and the eight-inch gap between the top of a caged enclosure and the ceiling. At some libraries he had shinnied up the cable of the book dumbwaiter to get from open areas to restricted ones. "I'm pretty sharp about that," Blumberg said. One time he removed a panel on a service-elevator shaft to get into the shaft and had begun climbing when the elevator started up. He had had to press himself into an inspection bay in the wall to avoid being crushed.

One of Blumberg's favorite targets was the library system at Harvard. To gain access to the Widener Library, he stole an identification card from a professor at the University of Minnesota and used it to secure a ninety-day library stack pass. With this, he was able to get into the stacks and, wearing an overcoat with large interior pockets, smuggled in a pair of horseshoe-nail pullers. "Blumberg used the tool to remove a lock cylinder, replaced the cylinder with a blank he'd brought with him, then took the boosted cylinder around to locksmiths," Weiss writes.

Blumberg explained to Weiss, " 'It was a Russell and Irwin lock. This key series was restricted in Boston, and I had to go all the way to Montreal before I could get it.' When he finally found the master, he went back to Harvard and replaced his blank. 'After that I went wherever the staff went—the key worked on all the offices.' "

The books Blumberg stole included *A Confession of Faith,* the first book printed in Connecticut in 1610; the 1493 *Nuremberg Chronicle,* bound in ivory calfskin; a Bible from 1480; and three shelves of priceless material from 1450 to 1500. He removed any identifying library or bookstore marks from the books, which made returning them to their rightful owners once he was caught a nightmare for the FBI.

Blumberg's arrest in 1990 came as a result of his "friend" Kenneth Rhodes, who became an undercover agent for the FBI. Rhodes and Blumberg had known each other since the mid-1970s, and Rhodes accompanied Blumberg on several of his book heists. Rhodes turned him in for a $56,000 reward.

Weiss notes, "Documents in Blumberg's possession at the time of his 1990 arrest included a listing of university special collections, floor plans of two buildings, and newspaper clippings about the holdings of various libraries. Rhodes, the former associate, said Blumberg was an expert locksmith, who would case the library during the day and return at night for the books." According to Kenny Rhodes in a 1991 issue of the *Abbey Newsletter,* "It was his [Blumberg's] habit to read constantly through the night, catnapping, waking, reading, dozing, waking, reading again, never fully sleeping."

At Blumberg's 1991 trial, Dr. William S. Logan, director of law and psychiatry at the Menninger Clinic and a nationally recognized authority on forensic psychiatry, revealed Blumberg had undergone treatment for schizophrenic delusions and tendencies and had been hospitalized numerous times during his adolescence. Dr. Logan also revealed that there was a history of psychiatric illness in Blumberg's family.

The FBI asked Paul Kisselburg, who by then owned Harold's Books, to come to Omaha, Nebraska, and identify any books Blumberg might have stolen from Harold's. Even though Blumberg had removed all the identifying marks from the books, he wrote his own code in some of them. The code for Harold's was "Old Hickory." Paul was able to recover about fifty books—a far cry from the hundreds that had been stolen. Blumberg was sentenced to five years in prison and fined $200,000 in July of 1991. After serving four and a half years, he was released but continued burglarizing houses and was arrested again in 1997 and 2004.

My contact with John Jenkins came when he ordered some unusual Texas books that I had listed in one of my weekly catalogs. He ordered several and promised to send a check the following day. I'd heard of Jenkins, who was from Austin, Texas, because he had been the president of the Antiquarian Booksellers' Association of America (ABAA)[3] from 1980 to 1982 and was widely regarded as one of the premier book dealers in the country. For a lowly bookseller like me, this was like getting a call from the king of England.

In a book about his exploits called *Audubon and Other Capers: Confessions of a Texas Bookmaker,* Jenkins described how, in 1971, he had helped the FBI track down some criminals with ties to the New York Mafia. These mobsters had stolen a valuable portfolio of engravings by the naturalist and

[3] I never joined the ABAA, following the old Mark Twain adage that I wouldn't want to belong to any organization that would have me as a member.

artist John James Audubon from Union College in New York and tried to sell them to Jenkins. Jenkins—who also had a law degree from the University of Texas—realized they were stolen and contacted the FBI, which enlisted him in an undercover sting to help recover the engravings. This case catapulted him into the upper echelons of book dealers in Texas.

In another caper, as he called them, Jenkins describes selling over five hundred thousand items worth $30 million to the University of Texas and other institutions. When he paid $10 million for the Eberstadt Collection, an archive of Texas and western territory history, he got even more publicity. But Jenkins was as notorious for drinking, gambling, and womanizing as he was for buying and selling books. He played high-stakes poker in Las Vegas in the early 1980s and was known on the circuit as "Austin Squatty" for his unusual habit of sitting at the tables perched on a chair with his legs crossed beneath him. Jenkins was barely five foot six, and to compensate for his short stature he wore cowboy boots made of ostrich and snake skins with three-inch heels. He wore a Stetson cowboy hat, smoked big cigars, and sometimes came to the poker tables wearing a full-length mink coat.

Jenkins was actually a pretty good poker player. In a 2009 article, Storms Reback reported, "Between 1983 and 1987, he won $155,855 in a variety of tournaments in Las Vegas. He made three final tables at the World Series of Poker, including a seventh-place finish at the main event in 1983, and played marathon poker sessions that lasted for days. He wore a gaudy Rolex watch, carried around large amounts of cash, and he played lots and lots of golf, even though, by most accounts, he couldn't hit the ball very far." Jenkins lost most of the money he made playing poker gambling on golf, and his odds weren't helped by his heavy drinking. Once he got so drunk on a golf course he dropped two $5,000 bundles of cash and didn't realize they were missing until he woke up the next morning. Everyone else must have been drinking too, because when he went back to look for the money, he found the cash in a sand trap by the eighteenth green.

The ABAA put the fox in charge of the hen house when it made Jenkins its head of security in 1982. A pamphlet he wrote called *Rare Books and Manuscript Thefts: A Security System for Librarians, Booksellers and Collectors* claimed that book thieves could be classified into five different types: the Kleptomaniac, the Thief Who Steals for Himself, the Thief Who Steals in Anger, the Casual Thief, and the Thief Who Steals for Profit. Book thieves, he maintained, "tend to exhibit classifiable characteristics."

Jenkins's knowledge of this criminal behavior was more than theoretical. He'd been stealing books from libraries and buying stolen merchandise almost from the day he became a bookseller. Later, he branched out into insurance fraud. The warehouse where he kept his rare books, for instance, kept burning down, and on two occasions he collected millions of dollars in damages.[4] After the warehouse caught fire a third time, his insurance company suspected arson and wouldn't pay. Jenkins wasn't charged, but the ABAA got fed up with all the bad publicity and kicked him out of the organization in 1988, noting that his footprints had been found at the scene of one of the fires and that the premises were unusually well insured. During one of the arson investigations it was also discovered that Jenkins possessed some forged documents, including several copies of the very rare Texas Declaration of Independence.

In his book *Texfake: An Account of the Theft and Forgery of Early Texas Printed Documents,* W. Thomas Taylor noted

---

[4] Later accounts noted that he moved his truly rare items before these conflagrations.

that in 1970 there were only five known copies of the Texas Declaration of Independence in existence, but by the mid-1980s almost twenty had turned up. Curious, Taylor examined every copy he could find and determined that only ten were legitimate. The others, with their fuzzier type and narrower columns, were forgeries. By tracing these back to their sources, he found that every fake declaration had been sold by one of three Texas dealers: John Jenkins, William Simpson, or Dorman David. (Dorman David appears again later in our narrative, and not in a good way.)

A 2006 article in the *Texas Observer* quoted appraiser C. Wesley Cowan: "These fakes fooled a lot of people for a long time. The one person who finally admitted to faking the documents, long after the fact, was Dorman David. Jenkins and Simpson always maintained that they had no knowledge that anything they sold was a forgery. Some of the documents Jenkins sold to the University of Texas were forged and it's likely that he knowingly sold several fakes of the Texas Declaration of Independence."

Things went from bad to worse for Jenkins when the Federal Deposit Insurance Corporation (FDIC) sued him for fraud in 1989 in connection with a $1.3 million loan that he'd taken out to finance a wildcat drilling operation. Then things got way worse. On April 16, 1989, Jenkins was found dead floating on a stretch of the Colorado River between Austin and Bastrop, Texas. All the evidence pointed to murder: he had been shot in the back of the head, the passenger-side door of his gold Mercedes was found ajar, and all his cash and credit cards were missing from his wallet. Still, Con Keirsey, the sheriff of Bastrop County, ruled the death a suicide.

"To explain why a gun was never found at the scene of the crime, Keirsey created what came to be known as 'the plastic-Coke-bottle theory,' " wrote Storms Reback. "He believed

Jenkins attached the gun he used to a large plastic Coke bottle riddled with holes. After shooting himself, Jenkins dropped the bottle into the river, and it floated downstream until it filled with water and sank." Perhaps, by staging his suicide as a murder, Jenkins wanted to defraud his insurance company one last time, but there were plenty of people who might have wanted him dead. He hung out with unsavory characters, both in the poker world and the world of book thieves and forgers.

As James E. McWilliams noted in an article in the *Texas Observer* in 2006, Jenkins's life captured the spirit of the age: "Jenkins, whose addictions so tragically bled into each other, captured in extreme form many of the qualities that made rare book dealing such a rush before the digital age—the hunt, the gamble, the ego, the intrigue, the competitiveness, the grand gesture, and, maybe more than anything else, the precious worth of individually accumulated knowledge." Kevin Mac-Donnell, who managed Jenkins's literary first editions from 1980 to 1986, summed up his life this way to McWilliams: "John Jenkins worked harder to make a dishonest dollar than an honest one, but he was a great bookman."

Jenkins's check to me, by the way, cleared.

To bring my exposure to book criminals a little more current— and skipping over several other examples—in 2018 it was discovered that John Schulman, the owner of Caliban Book Shop in Pittsburgh, and Gregory Priore, the head archivist at the Carnegie Library of Pittsburgh, had conspired in a twenty-year scheme to steal books, maps, and plates from the library worth an estimated $8 million. This was one of the largest rare book thefts from a single library in American history.

In my traveling days, I would go out of my way to go to Caliban's, one of the great secondhand bookstores in the country.

Schulman was a pleasant, subdued guy who once invited me to look at the books in his warehouse. They were amazing: early atlases, important books from the 1600s, rare botanicals—stuff you usually only see in auction catalogs. To a journeyman bookseller like me, who spent his time buying ten-dollar books and selling them for twenty, it was a depressing display of the rarities real rare booksellers handled.

Schulman's co-conspirator, Priore, was in charge of the Carnegie Library's repository of rare books, called the Oliver Room. On orders from Schulman, he would either steal books or cut out valuable maps and prints and bring these to Caliban's—a block away from the library—on his way home from work. When the crime was uncovered, Priore was found to have received fifty one checks from Schulman, worth $117,000.

According to Karen Yuan in the *Atlantic*:

> Priore and Schulman used an official library stamp to mark books as "withdrawn"—legitimately taken from the collection and cleared for sale. Schulman allegedly forged a withdrawal confirmation letter using Carnegie Library letterhead provided to him by Priore. Other books they "cannibalized," or cut out valuable parts to sell, with Priore stowing the leftover bindings on high shelves, where they were apparently safe from detection. Their actions weren't discovered until April 2017, when the library conducted an audit of the Oliver Room's collection and discovered missing items. Before that, the collection hadn't been audited since 1991, a year before Priore became responsible for it.

This was a shocking crime. Schulman was one of the premier book dealers in the country—he had operated Caliban's for nearly thirty years, appraised books on *Antiques Roadshow,* and served on the ABAA's board of governors, where he was in charge of its ethics committee. Travis McDade, who is a specialist in library book thefts, writes in *Thieves of Book Row* that Schulman and Priore's arrangement was quite unusual. Normally, librarians who steal books sell them to unsuspecting dealers; they don't work with them. After the crime came to light, there was plenty of hemming and hawing about how the library should have had better security and how Schulman betrayed his sacred trust as a rare book dealer, but it came down to the two usual suspects: opportunity and greed. Priore had money problems, and Schulman offered him a solution. It would be interesting to know how the subject of stealing books even came up between these two respected members of the book community.

The pair stole a total of 314 items from the Oliver Room, some printed as early as 1477. They included a first edition of Isaac Newton's *Principia* (a copy of which sold for $3.7 million in 2016), a first edition of Adam Smith's *The Wealth of Nations,* and a first folio edition of Edmund Spenser's classic poem *The Faerie Queene,* published in London in 1609. They also took numerous other atlases, maps, and large-plate books. "This was a magnificent collection that would cover the entire breadth of Western civilization. Spenser's poem alone is a landmark in literature," said Michael Vinson, a rare book dealer who reviewed the list of stolen books for the library.

Priore and Schulman were charged with theft and conspiracy in 2018 and pled guilty to the crimes in 2020. Almost as shocking as the crime was the sentence they received: three and four years of house arrest, respectively, and twelve years of probation. Schulman only had to pay $55,000 in restitution for his part in damaging and stealing $8 million worth of books.

5. A Book Fair
with the General

A book is a mirror; if an ass peers into it,
you can't expect an apostle to peer out.
GEORG CHRISTOPH LICHTENBERG

A COUPLE OF DOORS DOWN from me was the antique store
owned by Carrie, an older woman who'd been there for
years. When I needed a diversion, I visited Carrie. She had some
kind of nerve condition that made her shout "Ow!" whenever
you talked to her. She was full of doom and gloom about the
antique business and talked about how she could barely pay
her rent because business was so bad. Her husband, Tom, was
an old smoker, rail thin with sunken cheeks and a raspy voice,
who sat in an overstuffed lounge chair at the back of the store.
He would look like he was sleeping, but whenever a customer
picked up something, like a piece of glassware or an antique
toy, one eye would pop open and he'd say, "We can do better
on that for you."

Frank did give me one piece of good advice when he said,
"The true bookseller is not bound by the whims of the walk-in
customer." After being at the store for a few weeks I realized
that what he really meant was that I wasn't going to *have* any
walk-in customers. The only way I could make money was
through the mail, so my daily obsession became searching the
AB Bookman's Weekly for books I could sell that I either had
in the store or could buy from other booksellers. This was
the best, and only, education in the book business I ever got.

I learned what books people wanted and what they would pay for them. Given my desperate straits, I only bought books I knew people were looking for.

This was different from most of the old-guard booksellers, who started as book scouts, worked at used bookstores, or developed personal collections. They often bought books in bunches. They weren't indiscriminate about this—condition, whether it was a book club or ex-library, whether it was an obviously common title, and so on were factors—but their approach was much broader than mine. People brought books to the store, or the bookseller would get called to a house, and once the transaction was complete the householder would say, "Just take the rest." How tempting. What a godsend. Free books. Usually, though, free books are, in the vernacular, dogs, and the cumulative effect of having too many of these mutts in a store is pernicious.

I have gone into stores just starting out, where everything is in order, the books lined up on the shelves just so, the owner proud and optimistic. By the next year, the store has taken in every stray in the neighborhood and is a mess, with a ratty, substandard stock. The owner is behind the desk, depressed, shifting this junk around for the hundredth time. I always felt that every book I handled cost me money—in storage, time, and effort—no matter how I got it. In my later years, when people asked me for advice about getting into the book business, one thing I would tell them was that there's no such thing as a free book.

Even after five years, though, my store was more like a hobby than an actual business.[1] I was buying books and im-

---

[1] This was 1987, and I also had my fourth child, Jonathan, that year. I had junked my $200 Volvo and now drove a 1974 Volkswagen station wagon. This was red and rusty and had an old-style dashboard. For a junker, I thought it looked pretty good. The wipers worked on that car, but

proving the stock, but the quotes I sent out barely covered my expenses. I lay awake nights thinking of ways to sell more books. As I tossed and turned, I realized that the only people making money in mail order were the book search people. Those greedy criminals. They'd buy a book from me for five dollars and sell it for twenty-five. But they were still in business, and I almost wasn't. What if, I wondered, I became a book searcher myself, but for people who went to new bookstores? A few large book search operations dominated the scene then, and bookstores did searches for people who walked in the door, but it was a closed system—most book searches were done by used booksellers for used book people.

To put the book search business in perspective, you'll recall that the *AB Bookman's Weekly* began in 1948 as a way to find out-of-print books. In 1952 *The New Yorker* did a lengthy profile called "Book Scout" about a man named Louis Scher that provides a window into the origins of the organized book search business. "There are a great many indigents on the fringes of the secondhand book trade who call themselves scouts," the article begins, "but there are perhaps no more than a dozen men in America who can make book-scouting pay." By its later definition, Scher wasn't really a book scout but a book searcher, because he already had customers for many of the books he bought and charged premium prices for them.

Scher kept fifty thousand books in stock and ran his business out of a warehouse that he called the Seven Bookhunters.[2] "Ike Brussel ... who refers to himself as the last of the 'old-time scouts' (he scorns anyone who has an office or a staff), once

---

I still brought the battery into the house when the temperature got below zero, which, in Minnesota, was often.

[2] Only two people actually worked there, but Scher thought seven sounded better.

remarked that Scher's stock consisted mostly of 'morning glories'—books temporarily in demand but of no lasting value—and indeed it is hard to think how else to class, for example, Rudolph Valentino's *How to Keep Fit* (a book written in 1923 . . . and illustrated with pictures of the actor in swimming trunks), which the Seven Bookhunters sold to a woman in New Jersey for fifty dollars after buying it for two dollars a week before."

Scher had a prodigious memory for books, but he was no scholar: "He practically never reads the literary treasures he unearths; he is crazy about watching prizefights and baseball and puts in a good many hours at his neighborhood pool hall . . . Most scouts limit themselves to one or two specialties . . . but Scher keeps many flagrantly unscholarly titles in his head. He knows he can sell them at a profit if he can find them."

The article also describes how much Scher traveled looking for books. He was out hunting for six months of the year and covered between fifteen and twenty thousand miles annually, often by train. "He has four main circuits: the Boston trip, which he makes twice a year; the Washington and Chicago trips, both of which he makes three times a year; and the West Coast trip, which he makes once a year." Since he traveled by train, he stopped at all the cities in between. "Many conductors were outraged by the way Scher squeezed the utmost out of his transportation dollar, and when—as sometimes happened—[his ticket] fell apart in their hands, their scorn was so withering that only a man like Scher could survive it."

Anyway, I decided to get into the book search business myself, but to do that I needed customers. I figured people looking for out-of-print books at new bookstores were like me before I went into the Arcade Street store: they didn't realize they could only get those books from secondhand booksellers. In my pitch to the new bookstores, I told them that by farming out their book requests to me, they could offer a free service and, as a bonus, get the people who came in every Saturday asking for Elsie Dinsmore books off their backs.

I was amazed such a simple idea worked so well. For every hundred letters I sent out, about twenty stores responded. Before long, the search requests came pouring in, and I started advertising for long lists of books in the *AB Bookman's Weekly*. I got requests for books so common I could walk into any used bookstore and find three copies on the shelf and another seven in the back room. On other books, I'd get a hundred or more quotes, some for as low as a dollar. When I found a book, the customer almost always bought it. Some were so grateful that more than one called it a "miracle."[3]

The book search idea worked, in part, because regular people were either unaware of or reluctant to go into used bookstores. The stores tended to be in out-of-the-way places. They could be seedy and chaotic, their owners crotchety and hostile. Many booksellers would buy books from every lowlife who walked through the door but could be high-handed when it came to selling them: their customers were collectors and academics, not the common man or woman. Some were even fussy about

---

[3] Another idea I had around this time was to call Goodwill and offer my services as a book expert: I would tell them what to save from the books they received in donations, and in return they would let me buy any books I wanted for $1 each. They loved the idea. I would go to a warehouse in St. Paul every week and sort through these bins full of books. It was nasty work and could take a full day, but boy, did I find some good stuff. A couple that stand out are a first edition of *Tarzan of the Apes* by Edgar Rice Burroughs, which I immediately sold to another dealer for $300; it would sell for $4,000 today. Another was *Profiles in Courage,* signed by John F. Kennedy, which I sold through the mail for $1,250 but would sell for $15,000 now.

the books they would handle; books favored by the unwashed masses, like how Elvis was living somewhere in Argentina, were beneath them. With four kids to support, I couldn't afford to be so particular, so if I knew someone would pay forty-five dollars to find out if Elvis liked dulce de leche in his old age, I'd buy the book. A few preferred to be called "bookmen" and regarded selling rare or collectible books to commoners as crass, almost dishonest, because people were not sophisticated enough to know the value of what they were buying.

Once the book search business got going, business improved enough for me to think about quitting the hospital job. When I brought this up to Mary Pat, she was surprised things might be getting better and not, as usual, worse. Somehow, I convinced her that selling used books full-time from a rat hole in St. Paul was better than having a stable job, so in 1987—after thirteen years of dealing with troubled adolescents, with four children to support and a balance of forty-two dollars in my checking account—I quit my day job. Like the old Samuel Johnson quote that says that when a man is about to be hanged, "it concentrates his mind wonderfully," my only focus now was making enough money to support my family.

It's an axiom in the used book business that if you aren't out buying books, you're going out of business, so to be successful I knew I needed to cover a wider range than the local estate sales, library sales, and occasional dead bookseller. Luckily, I met Paul Kisselburg around this time, a military book collector who became my best bookseller friend and longtime traveling companion.

At first Paul and I traveled around the Midwest, but eventually we covered most of the United States, Canada, and England. These trips were supposed to be mutually beneficial, but Paul, who had money and a van, only picked places where he could find military books, so he skimmed the cream while I collected the scraps. Paul, it pains me to say, displayed a callous disregard for my personal comfort and business needs on our trips together, and this grew steadily worse as the years went by.

To take just one example, I called Paul "the General" because he collected military books, but also because he kept a rigid and, some would say, inhumane travel schedule. If I have kidney problems now—and I'm not saying I do—it is because Paul would refuse to even stop at a restroom as we barreled down the road in his hideous green van. He claimed he had a strict itinerary and no time for frivolities like bathroom breaks, but I believed there was an element of perverse cruelty in this as well. Still, he did pay for the gas and had the van to haul books in, so I put up with his indignities.

Paul's interest in military books stemmed from his college studies in history, but in the depressed 1980s his first job after college was on the railroad, where he traveled from Minnesota to Iowa chasing away train hoppers. While riding the rails he also worked part time for some Twin Cities book dealers, including Melvin McCosh, Harold Lensing, and Jim Laurie.

As Paul describes it, "For about a year, while I worked full-time on the railroad, I worked one day a week at McCosh's. I cleaned rooms and alphabetized books. He and I would then spend one or two hours over lunch every day talking about the book business. That is where I learned so much. I learned about the 'good' people and the 'bad' people in the business—from his point of view, of course. I learned much about authors and subjects that he did well in. He loved to cook. Always needed money."

Paul worked on the railroad until 1983 and then became an air traffic controller. In 1986 he bought Harold's Books in downtown St. Paul with his "real" friend Ted Henry, who worked in construction during the day but in his off-hours collected books about actors and the cinema. Paul would buy books for Harold's, but—unbeknownst to Ted, who was paying half his expenses—spent as much time, or more, adding to his own military book collection. Even then, through Harold's and his collecting, Paul was a major player on the Minnesota bookselling scene.

In 1988, Paul and I started going to Chicago—the center of the book world in the Midwest then—nearly every month to buy books. We got to know the dealers there as well as, or better than, we knew those in the Twin Cities. In October 1988 we were invited to exhibit at the book fair sponsored by the Midwest Antiquarian Booksellers Association—called, for short, the Midwest Bookhunters—being held that month at Northwestern University. The popularity of book fairs, like most things associated with used books, has declined in the modern era, but the Midwest Bookhunters still manage to put on two every year, one in Chicago and one in Minneapolis.

These book fairs follow a tradition that began long before there were printed books. In the thirteenth century, a trade fair that sold handwritten manuscripts was held every year in Frankfurt, Germany. After Gutenberg invented the printing press in 1440, two of his employees started a competing fair that included printed books. This became the primary place for bookselling in Germany, for both printed books and handwritten texts. Reminiscent of the way modern booksellers regard the internet is the reaction in 1458 to the invention of printing by Vespasiano da Bisticci, a well-known Florence bookseller and manuscript dealer. He was "so outraged that books would no longer be written out by hand that he closed his shop in a fit of rage and became the first person in history to prophesy the death of the book industry," wrote Jen Campbell in *The Bookshop Book.*

According to Nicholas Basbanes in *A Gentle Madness,* Vespasiano was technically the first publisher and commercial bookseller. He mass-produced handwritten books for Cosimo de' Medici in the mid-1400s and helped Pope Nicholas V assemble the Vatican's manuscript collection. All the books he sold, though, "had to be written with the pen," Vespasiano recalled years later, as "anything else would have made the collector feel ashamed."

"Within twenty years of the invention of printing—about 1465—books became so accessible that even the poorest scholars could afford them," wrote Rosenbach in *Books and Bidders.* "Tracts of various kinds were marketed for a few pennies which at first had sold for pounds. There was so much printing done that some printers were ruined because the supply quickly outgrew the demand. When, in the latter part of the fifteenth century, Italian noblemen saw how common printing had become, they regarded it as vulgar. Although they had at first been the patrons of printing, now some of them ignored it and endowed scriptoriums, in the hope that printing would fall into disfavor."

By 1480, printing presses in over one hundred European cities were cranking out books willy-nilly. A Venice scribe complained that the city was stuffed with books. Nicholas Basbanes writes that "conferences and book fairs were held, trends were surveyed, and sales strategies were developed. The first known author's copyright was issued . . . in 1486."

Exhibiting at book fairs took a lot of time and cost a lot of money. The fairs ran from one to three days and the dealers had to bring in bookcases, tables, signs, and anywhere from thirty to a hundred boxes of books. For our first fair at Northwestern, Paul and I decided to build an enormous five-foot-tall by fifteen-foot-wide pine bookcase to display our books—close to half the shelving in my Arcade Street store—in Paul's garage. Paul was too cheap to buy the small folding bookcases most booksellers used and, of course, blamed me when this bookcase became a liability.

When the time for the fair came, we loaded that fifteen-foot monstrosity and a hundred boxes of our best books into Paul's van. When we got to Northwestern, we lugged the whole works across campus, past curious students and academics, to the conference center where the book fair was being held. With two thousand books on it, this case was so unstable it was scary; it swayed like a badly built suspension bridge in a high wind. This weird-looking contraption alerted the other dealers that we were beginners, and that meant bargains, so they swarmed our booth and tore through our boxes like buzzards on a dead zebra before we could even get set up.

The real action at book fairs took place between the dealers. A book might be marked up three or four times before it ever reached a customer. At the Northwestern fair, for example, one dealer had a first edition of one of the books in the Wizard of Oz series by L. Frank Baum—inscribed by Baum to his mother, no less. This was one of the author's later titles (the original *Wonderful Wizard of Oz* in good condition can sell for over $50,000) and was priced at $3,000. Another dealer bought it and marked it up to $4,500. A second dealer bought the same book and marked it up to $6,000. It went through two more dealers before it was finally sold to a regular customer for $14,000, much to the consternation of the dealer who had it in the first place.

We took that bookcase to two more fairs, one at DePaul University and one at Printer's Row in downtown Chicago.

The book fair. Courtesy Midwestern Antiquarian Booksellers Association.

After the Printer's Row fair, while we were carrying it back to the van—Paul complaining about it all the while—we saw a dumpster and, well, dumped it.

Even then, in the late 1980s, there were signs of changes in the book business. As Paul notes, "By the late '80s, university libraries were losing interest in books. I remember our MWBH [Midwest Bookhunters] fairs at Northwestern. MWBH gave a large gift to the university library each year in appreciation of letting us have the fair there. MWBH tried to find a way to give the library even more value by increasing the size of the gift if the library used the money to purchase books from MWBH dealers. No deal. The library did not want books. It wanted cash for computers."

6. Bookman's Alley
and McCosh's Mansion

That's it then. This is how it ends.
And I haven't even read Proust yet.
JAMES TURNER, *Rex Libris*

A T BOOK FAIRS the personalities of the booksellers were on full display. Their odd quirks and fierce independence were an integral part of the business. The big shots—the rare book dealers—displayed their books in fancy glass cases while the low-end guys put out their beat-up stuff in cardboard boxes. If you didn't like the way they ran things, too bad. These offbeat, sometimes eccentric people were part of what made the business so interesting. John Jenkins and A. S. W. Rosenbach gained fame from their exploits buying and selling books but are also remembered for their larger-than-life personalities. Even the booksellers who died in squalid circumstances, like Morris and Malcolm—God rest their souls— were such characters that they were talked about long after they were gone.

With the internet the bookseller's ability to put a personal stamp on their businesses has changed. As Paul Kisselburg puts it, "In the past, a book dealer had an identity. He named his shop after himself, e.g., Harold's Bookshop, Kisselburg Military Books, etc. The internet has taken this from them. When we had stores, the businesses we created reflected the tastes and idiosyncrasies of the owners."

So let's take another break here and look at how the personalities of a couple of booksellers reflected the way they did business. Among the many possible subjects for this, I have chosen Roger Carlson from Chicago and Melvin McCosh from Minneapolis, two booksellers who could not have been more different. Roger was polished and cultured, drove a used Mercedes, and hobnobbed with Chicago's upper crust. Melvin was abrupt and eccentric, wore a rope for a belt, and lived alone in a run-down mansion filled with half a million books. Both, though, had a profound impact on the secondhand book businesses in their respective cities. It could be said of them what Shakespeare said in *Hamlet*: "He was a man, take him for all in all, I shall not look upon his like again."

Roger was the owner of Bookman's Alley—so called because it was down an alley—in Evanston, Illinois. This store was a showpiece, a welcoming gathering place that captured the spirit of the Chicago book trade in the late '80s and early '90s. Roger was originally from Minneapolis, where he sold advertising before deciding to pursue his childhood dream of opening a bookstore. When he was fifty, he bought a dilapidated building in Evanston and built up his business while he survived on money he'd saved from his advertising days. He told me it took him eight years working seventy-five-hour weeks before he made a living selling books.

In an article in *Book Source Monthly* by Carlos Martinez, Roger described his bookselling philosophy. "During the first years I did a number of things to attract customers," he said. "We had pianists, string quartets, blues singers, and twenty-five or thirty book auctions. We hosted a wedding, a wake, a marriage proposal—accepted—and a small number of author signings. The pleasure of a shop for me was in large part the common interest I shared with a large percentage of my patrons. In my thirty-two years of operating the shop I have come to know hundreds of regulars, and I remember most of them with some degree of affection."

Roger said he wanted a bookstore that didn't have the "same atmosphere as a soup kitchen. I was dressing the set, if you think of my shop as a presentation." So Bookman's Alley was decorated with antiques and curiosities from his years of collecting: trophies, sporting equipment, an original framed letter by Dorothy Parker, military uniforms, a piano, a chalkboard listing the best sellers from 1980. If there was an old western saddle you knew you were in the Western Americana section. Aviator goggles on a mannequin and model airplanes strung up on the ceiling meant you were in Aviation. It was a show. Roger had more books than he knew what to do with, but the sections in his store were never crowded, and he always kept two or three rare or unusual books on display. Most frustrating for traveling booksellers were the stacks of unpriced books covered with blankets scattered throughout the store.

Roger Carlson, Bookman's Alley, Evanston, Illinois.
Photograph copyright Marc Perlish.

Roger was a true gentleman. Funny, intelligent, and down to earth. He gained a measure of fame when Audrey Niffenegger used his shop as a setting in her novel *The Time Traveler's Wife,* and it was also included in the documentary *Finding Vivian Maier,* about a nanny and sometime customer who took tens of thousands of photographs of Chicago street scenes. In 2012, he wanted to sell the store and retire but had trouble finding a buyer: "Operating a bookshop involves a vow of poverty. The shop has a number of strong negatives," he said. "The building has no plumbing and lacks central air. The big boxes, the internet, and the reading machines have combined to make this business something of a crapshoot." Roger's store truly reflected his personality—charming, witty, and high class. He closed it in 2013, partly because of the internet and partly due to health problems. Roger died in 2017 at the age of eighty-nine.

In Minnesota, the radical iconoclast Melvin McCosh sent out fliers every three months or so inviting people to come to his "House of Books" on Lake Minnetonka in Excelsior. This flyer included a hand-scrawled list of the subjects covered in his stock of nearly half a million books and concluded with "You need these books more than I do."

McCosh opened his first bookstore in 1952 on the porch of his house in Minneapolis. Later he opened a store in an old house in Dinkytown, near the University of Minnesota. One of his early customers was Bob Dylan, a Minnesota native who lived near the university from 1959 to 1960. In his autobiography, *Chronicles: Volume I,* Dylan writes, "Pankake [a friend of Dylan's] lived in an apartment above McCosh's bookstore, a place that specialized in eclectic old books, ancient texts, philosophical political pamphlets from the 1800s on up. It was a neighborhood hangout for intellectuals and Beat types, on the main floor of an old Victorian house."

A customer recalled in an online forum that McCosh was never fond of Dylan. "In general, he wasn't very well liked at all," he said of the musician. "He was sort of pompous. To be fair, I'd like to say something good about him, but I can't think of anything right now." McCosh also told the story of how "Dylan was playing poker above Gray's Campus Drug when a fire truck went by. The other players got up and looked out the window to see where the truck was going, and when they looked back, Dylan was gone—and so was the money."

"During those years [in Dinkytown], the flamboyant Mc-Cosh sometimes wore a raccoon coat, red Snoopy sunglasses and had a handlebar mustache. He had a succession of big dogs, all named White Dog, and he was a gourmet cook who boasted that he was one of the few non-natives who liked lutefisk," recounted the *Pioneer Press* in 2007. McCosh's acerbic sense of humor was legendary around the university. Every year at homecoming, he'd put a scrawled sign in the store window telling the alumni to go home. But his supporters were fervent. When rumors spread that Bridgeman's wanted to expand into the bookstore's space, students blocked off the intersection and staged "sip-ins," monopolizing space at the ice cream store.

As Dinkytown became more popular and developers moved in, McCosh was forced to relocate, first to an old firehouse on the West Bank and then out of Minneapolis altogether. In 1971, he bought a run-down building on Lake Minnetonka and filled its forty-two rooms with books. It had been built in the early 1900s, when wealthy bankers, industrialists, and flour barons—with names like Pillsbury, Cargill, and Brooks—took advantage of the new rail lines that ran from Minneapolis to spend summers at the lake.

The summer "cottages" they built were massive structures of forty to a hundred rooms, like Downton Abbey, with the family's

Melvin's mansion and the bookseller in his kitchen.
Photographs copyright Daniel Kramer.

living quarters on the upper floors and the servants' down below. They were constructed by armies of craftspeople and featured hand-carved woodwork, stained-glass windows, and stone floors that would cost millions in today's dollars.

McCosh likely didn't spend a dime improving or maintaining his building from the time he moved there to the time I went there in 1989. Paul says, "He had bought the building and many acres, some of which were on the lake. He did not need the lake frontage and sold that off. Of course, that lake frontage became exceptionally valuable. He could have solved his financial problems several times over if he had been able to keep that excess land and sell it in the '90s. McCosh would be open to the public about three or four times a year. That is when he would send out the famous fliers. People came from all over. It was a big deal."

Melvin McCosh was, in 1989, tall and very thin, with white hair and a long, scraggly beard. He wore reading glasses that sat on the edge of his nose and, like many booksellers of his era, often wore a suit jacket. The one I remember was the herringbone type, with patches on the elbows, like those favored by college professors, but any concession to style ended there. His ragged pants had a rope for a belt, and his shoes looked like they'd been chewed on by his big white dog. He had chronic back problems—an occupational hazard for booksellers—and once told me his doctor said he was not supposed to lift more than two pounds.

The Minnetonka house was stone, two stories high, with twenty or so rooms on each level. The rooms were connected by stone-tile hallways and lit with dim, old-style lamps. Every room was shelved and full of books. The hallways, likewise, were crammed with books and boxes, stacked from floor to ceiling, so just a path led from room to room. The only empty room in the house was a sunporch with huge leaded-glass windows and carved oak moldings. This room still had some of its original wicker furniture, but there was so much water damage—that's why it was empty—that the walls were covered with mold and plaster was dropping from the ceiling.

Each room had books on a specific subject, so if you were interested in, say, foreign literature or American history, it had a room. Subjects no one was interested in, like bibliography, likely had two rooms. McCosh's books included obscure doctoral theses, textbooks, and outdated treatises, so it took real work to find anything decent. Paul remembers that McCosh had filled his attic with remainders—those books publishers dump on the market when they don't sell—that he listed in *Books in Print*. As Paul recalls, "Every library and most booksellers kept these reference books to find out if a book was still being printed, and McCosh did very well listing these remainders, but he did not really publish the books. In the early '80s, people complained and McCosh was delisted. That was a blow to his business."

When it was time to check out, you brought the books to McCosh, who sat at a small desk near the entrance. Since the books weren't priced, what McCosh charged was based on the gleam in his customer's eye. Despite owning half a million books and being desperate to sell them, he would not budge on these prices. If he said ten dollars, it was ten dollars, take it or leave it.

McCosh could be gruff and did not suffer fools gladly, so it might be surprising to learn that he put together an extensive collection of books on humor. Underneath all his bluster he was a kind and generous man who readily shared his vast knowledge with other booksellers. Melvin died in 2007 at the age of eighty.

7. Beating
the Bushes

In the reproof of chance
lies the true proof of men.
WILLIAM SHAKESPEARE, *Troilus and Cressida*

GOING TO THE NORTHWESTERN BOOK FAIR opened up a new way for me to sell books—instead of sitting at the store waiting for the mail while another East Sider walked by with a package of wienerwurst, I could take my books on the road. So I bought some folding bookcases and went to as many book fairs as I could. These had to be within driving distance, and I could only take what I could jam into my Volkswagen station wagon, but in 1989 I went to the Michigan Book Fair in Lansing, the Ann Arbor Book Fair, the Rocky Mountain Book and Paper Fair in Denver, and at least two more in Chicago. Every trip meant at least a week on the road away from my family, sleeping in the cheapest fleabags I could find, and eating bad food at truck stops and diners.

On the way to and from these fairs I bought books at bookstores and from the quoters, those often strange book hermits who answered the ads I placed in the *AB Bookman's Weekly*. I made a point of tracking them down because their books tended to be cheaper and less picked over than those at regular bookstores. This wasn't always easy. A good many were, let's face it, people with pathological hoarding disorders who lived in out-of-the-way, godforsaken places with houses, sheds, and barns filled with books. I called ahead, often from dark phone booths, and when I got to whatever shack or hovel or run-down mansion they lived in, they always seemed to have dogs. Mean dogs. More than once, I sat in my car and waited for someone to rescue me while a big dog slobbered at my driver's-side window.

These people were not used to visitors and often greeted me like a long-lost relative—many said I was the first regular book dealer to ever contact them. Their houses might have an organized workspace where they filled out the postcards they mailed every week, but the rest of the place would be a mess, with stacks of broken boxes and books piled everywhere. Any outbuildings would have books so jammed in they were impossible to get at.

One guy, who was probably seventy, insisted I stay for dinner and try the authentic Danish food his ninety-year-old mother was cooking. He told me his *moder* had slaved over the stove all day in anticipation of my visit, so I couldn't refuse the invitation. Now, I am no connoisseur of Danish cuisine, but to me the food was awful. There were creamed potatoes that looked and tasted like yellow Play-Doh and fish that smelled like turpentine. As I ate the mother and son watched me like I was a zoo animal, so of course I lied and said how great it all was. I never accepted another invitation to eat anywhere else again, ever.

Some of the more unusual collections I ever handled came from these stops at quoters' houses, and a few are worth describing, if only to illustrate how traveling booksellers rescued items of historical significance. In the basement of one house, for example, I came across a wooden box full of carefully organized photographic negatives. These were old negatives, the size of two-by-four-inch note cards, and there were hundreds of them. The quoter said that as far as he could tell they were pictures of a trip a couple took to Arizona. Mostly scenery. He wasn't interested in the negatives and was more than willing to sell the box. When I asked what he wanted for it, he said he'd take a hundred dollars.

I bought it and when I got back home looked through the negatives. They were fascinating. Notes with the pictures described a trip by car to Arizona in 1910 by a doctor and his wife who drove a rickety and temperamental car, with no support system along the way, through what was then wilderness. One picture was of the doctor changing a tire wearing goggles and a long duster. The car—I never did figure out what kind it was—regularly got stuck or hung up on trees and boulders. More important, though, were the pictures the couple took when they visited members of the Hopi tribe on the northeastern border of Arizona. There were pictures of adults, of children sitting on a dusty road, and of the Hopi snake dance, a ceremony the couple was able to document in considerable detail.

The snake dance is a religious ceremony that lasts for sixteen days in August and is performed by members of the Snake and the Antelope clans from all three of the mesas in that area of Arizona. The doctor's pictures showed the dancers capturing the poisonous snakes—like rattlesnakes—that they used in the snake dance and the elaborate washing rituals they engaged in before the ceremony. There were pictures of the dancers putting rattlesnakes between their teeth and then vomiting after drinking a potion said to remove any snake poison from their systems. These pictures were a few years earlier than the rare film taken of the Hopi snake dance when it was performed for Theodore Roosevelt on his visit to the Hopi tribe in 1913.

So this box of historically significant photographic negatives is sitting in my store on Arcade Street when another book dealer comes in and asks, "How much for the box?" I,

Hopi children, circa 1910.

desperate as always for money but not really wanting to sell the negatives, come up with a ridiculous price: $1,200, I say. You know what happens next. He buys the box and I regret the sale ever since. I did save twelve of the negatives and had them developed. One of the pictures, of the washing ritual of the snake dancers before the ceremony, is hanging in my son Steven's old bedroom, and I feel a sense of loss whenever I look at it.

On another trip, through Ohio, I stopped at the house of a man who, when he learned I was from Minnesota, asked if I'd ever heard of Ignatius Donnelly. All I knew about Donnelly was that he wrote some oddball books in the later 1800s on subjects like Atlantis and the Great Flood. I didn't even know he ever lived in Minnesota. It turned out this guy not only had written his master's thesis at the University of Minnesota on Ignatius

Donnelly but had a large collection of books and other materials about him that he wanted to sell.

Donnelly was, to put it mildly, an interesting character. He was born in Philadelphia in 1831, became a lawyer, and, after a rumored financial scandal, moved to Minnesota in 1852, when it was still a territory. With several investors, he started a utopian community called Nininger City on the banks of the Mississippi. When that failed, it left Donnelly deeply in debt. With no way to earn an honest living, he went into politics. In 1860 he was elected the first lieutenant governor of Minnesota. He then was elected to congress, where as a Radical Republican he supported the abolition of slavery, women's suffrage, and farmers' rights.

Donnelly left organized politics in 1878 but continued to speak out as a Populist about corruption in politics, fake newspaper reporting, and how people needed to "take back their country." In 1882, he published *Atlantis: The Antediluvian World,* which speculated that Atlantis, the underwater city described by Plato, was destroyed by the same flood that caused Noah to build his ark. His next book, *Ragnarok: The Age of Fire and Gravel,* claimed that the great flood, the destruction of Atlantis, and the extinction of the woolly mammoth were caused by the near collision of the earth with a massive comet. Both books sold very well and are, believe it or not, still in print. He claimed in another book that Francis Bacon was the author of Shakespeare's plays, and he regularly put out radical political pamphlets.

When Donnelly died in 1901, he was married to his second wife, a former secretary who was fifty years younger than he was. This master's thesis guy tracked the wife down in 1970—she was in her nineties by then—and taped their conversations. On the tapes, she talks in a halting voice about a man who died in 1901, seventy years before, like he could walk through the door at any minute. This guy also went to Nininger City and found Donnelly's abandoned house, which still contained what was left of his library: people would walk in and take whatever books they wanted or, in some cases, use Donnelly's books for target practice. I bought the collection (one book by Andrew Greeley still had a bullet slug lodged between the pages) and sold most of it to the Minnesota Historical Society, probably the only organization in the world that would get excited about those tapes and obscure political pamphlets.

Another quoter, in Springfield, Illinois, had a collection of books from the library of Albert Goodwill Spalding, an American pitcher, manager, and executive in the early years of professional baseball. He played major league baseball between 1871 and 1878 and reportedly was the first player to wear a baseball glove. After his playing days were over, he cofounded the Spalding sporting goods company and was president and part owner of the Chicago White Stockings. Spalding was instrumental in organizing the National League, wrote the first set of official baseball rules, and created a commission to study the origins of baseball. The commission didn't care for the game's connection to British cricket, so to lend an air of American patriotism to the game, it declared that Civil War general Abner Doubleday invented baseball in 1839.

An early book on baseball signed by A. G. Spalding would be worth its weight in gold. None of these books were about baseball, and very few were signed, but they all had Spalding's personalized stamp. I bought the signed books—an early archery book sold for a lot of money—and several of the stamped books. When I went to sell those, I was surprised to find that die-hard baseball collectors would still pay plenty for just Spalding's stamped name in a book.

8. A Bookstore
in Stillwater

*It is not the strongest of the species
that survives, but the most adaptable.*
LEON MEGGINSON

BY 1989, I was able, after a fashion, to support my wife
and children, but I was almost forty years old, lived in a
rented duplex, and had Colin, my fifth child, on the way. Our
East St. Paul neighborhood was changing: the Hamm's brew-
ery had closed, and Whirlpool had shipped most of its jobs to
Mexico. Meghan, our oldest, was in sixth grade and would
start junior high the next year, so Mary Pat and I decided to
move to Stillwater, a small town on the St. Croix River that we
often visited, twenty miles east of the Twin Cities on the border
of Wisconsin and Minnesota.

Coincidentally, around this time, Jim Cummings, who lived
in Stillwater, started coming to the Arcade Street store. Jim and
his wife, Kristen, had owned the Book House in Dinkytown in
Minneapolis, a large store (one hundred thousand–plus books)
that catered to the students at the University of Minnesota. Jim
traveled constantly buying stock for the store and books for his
personal collection of printed diaries. He was a bit obsessive—
buying books and stories about buying books consumed his
every waking hour—but you couldn't argue with his results.
Shortly after I met him, he left the Book House but still lived
in a Victorian mansion in Stillwater, where he kept his diary
collection and sold books through the mail.

Stillwater, Minnesota. Photograph by Jeff Lueders/Shutterstock.

In an article he wrote for the September 6, 1982, *AB Bookman's Weekly,* Jim says that his father got him interested in nature, collecting, and keeping a diary. When he was thirteen he began keeping a daily diary. He collected bird's nests, feathers, animal skulls, and turtle shells, and bought books by the naturalists John Muir and John Burroughs. In high school he collected books by the transcendental philosophers Emerson and Thoreau. After a hitch in the army and a brief stint at the University of Minnesota, he opened his first bookstore when he was twenty-five.

While cataloging and quoting books for his store, Jim noticed that printed diaries—those day-by-day accounts of, say, a soldier's battles in the Civil War or the trials of an Arctic explorer—sold well. That, and his own diary habit, sparked his interest in collecting diaries. By 1989 he had collected several thousand printed diaries, which he kept on the top floor of his mansion. In the *AB Bookman's Weekly* article, Jim says, "One tremendously appealing aspect of my diary collection is that it does cover all areas of life . . . just about any theme is touched on. There are diaries that are little more than account books. There are diaries kept in every region of this country and of the world. There are diaries kept by individuals whose entries are primarily important in such areas as anthropology, archaeology, architecture, art, book collecting, botany . . ." While some of these were just regular books, many were limited editions— signed by the authors or examples of fine book production. One leather-bound set I saw included a handwritten, signed letter from Ralph Waldo Emerson.

I started going to Jim's house in Stillwater to buy books for my weekly catalogs from the books he had for sale in his basement. We would talk about the business, especially the trials of running a bookstore. Jim told me that after owning the Book House for fifteen years and other stores for another ten, he was done selling books to the general public. He'd been doing it for twenty-five years and was tired of the cheapskates, tired of the hassle. No, it was going to be strictly mail order for him from then on. Still, while we were driving down the main street of downtown Stillwater, I saw a storefront for rent and Jim agreed it might be a good place for a bookstore.[1]

A week or two later, in what was nothing short of a miracle, a customer of mine, who we'll call Mike, walked into the Arcade Street store and asked if I had ever thought about selling my

---

[1] I looked for other places around the Twin Cities to open a store. I almost rented an old bar in St. Paul that was around the corner from another used bookstore, but the bar was in shambles, with water damage and who knows what other nightmares. I later learned that it had been built on the site of a gas station and auto repair shop so polluted that they had to spend nearly a half a million dollars just cleaning it up.

business. He was retired and wanted to become a gentleman bookseller.[2] I warned him that selling books from a rat hole in East St. Paul might look easy, but it wasn't. On the plus side, if he bought the store, I'd sell him three thousand of my four thousand books and teach him how to sell books through the mail. These were the books I had painstakingly acquired over the years and were hard to part with, but they would at least give Mike a fighting chance, which was more than I had when I bought the business from Frank in 1982.

We settled on a price of $10,000 for the books, the shelving, and the fixtures. Not much of a return for seven years of work, but Mike's offer was likely the only one I would ever get. After the sale was final, my first thought was that storefront for rent in Stillwater. It was where I thought a used bookstore should be. Regular people walked the streets there, searching for books from their childhoods or college days but unwilling to go to backwater secondhand stores so seedy only hard-core book freaks would dare walk through the doors. Jim agreed to contact the landlord of the store we'd seen—at 216 South Main Street—to look at the space. It was about 2,100 square feet, with a large front room and a smaller storage room in the back. The entrance and walk-in display windows were framed in old oak, and the entire store had a wood floor made of maple. It was a beautiful place.

Stillwater then was still a sleepy river town with traditional downtown businesses: clothing stores, a hardware store, a bakery, old-time cafés, and so on. The St. Croix River, which runs by the town, has been protected by the National Wild and Scenic Rivers Act since 1970, so the river today looks much like it did in 1683 when Father Louis Hennepin described it.

---

[2] In my experience, two mutually exclusive terms.

(Hennepin, by the way, was never there—he borrowed his description from someone else.) The settlers who first came to the area in the 1850s didn't come for the views, though. They came for the old-growth forests of white pine that covered 70 percent of Minnesota. Throughout the 1800s and into the 1900s, they cut down the trees and sent the logs down the St. Croix, where they were processed by the sawmills that lined the river.

People crossed the St. Croix first via ferry and later by a wooden pontoon bridge. In 1930, this was replaced by a steel lift bridge. For over eighty years that lift bridge was the only way to cross the river for miles on either side. In the summer it was raised every half hour to let big boats through, but it regularly broke down, and this caused frequent traffic jams. Beginning in 1950, a battle to replace it raged—brother against brother, conservationists against businesses—but a new bridge wasn't built until 2017. The historic lift bridge is now limited to pedestrian traffic and is one of the few of its kind left in the country.

A territorial convention to make Minnesota a state was held in Stillwater in 1848. As evidence of Stillwater's importance, the town was offered either the state capital or the state prison. Stillwater chose the prison so the local lumber companies could use convicts to work in the sawmills or tend logs as they floated down the river. The criminals were leased to the lumber companies, but eventually stories of abuse—prisoners being treated like slaves and put in situations that got them killed—reached the state legislature, and the practice was banned in 1895. The Stillwater prison was, for many years, the most secure facility in the state and held many notorious outlaws and gangsters over the years, including the Younger brothers, who robbed banks and trains with Jesse James.

The men who owned the lumber and the land along the

St. Croix made fortunes. They built large Victorian mansions on the hills of Stillwater and impressive red brick buildings—including the Grand Opera House—downtown. In *Stillwater: Minnesota's Birthplace,* Patricia Condon Johnston writes, "Stillwater's Grand Opera House was the finest in the Northwest. Illuminated by 101 ornate gas fixtures, the imposing auditorium accommodated twelve hundred patrons. For twenty years, some of the top road troupes in the country played the Grand Opera House. John Philip Sousa brought his world-famous band to Stillwater and prizefighters, including John L. Sullivan, appeared there."

The lumber barons thought the trees would last forever, but on August 12, 1914, the last log from the emptied pine forests floated down the St. Croix. Stillwater then entered a long period, from the 1920s to the 1980s, when it was just another unremarkable river town. By 1960, the population was half of what it had been in 1890. Nothing was happening in the town, so none of the old buildings were torn down. The Victorian mansions and red brick buildings were still there a hundred years later. When highway access improved and Stillwater began to promote its historical importance, tourists started coming, and the town started to wake up.

So opening a bookstore in downtown Stillwater wasn't a totally outlandish idea. After seeing the space on Main Street and noticing how many people walked by, Jim agreed that a bookstore in town might work, but he wanted to bring in a third partner to spread out the risk. This turned out to be Tom Loome, who also lived in Stillwater and who, along with his wife, Karen, owned Loome Theological Booksellers, the largest theological bookstore in the world with a stock of over 250,000 theology, philosophy, and medieval history books.

Tom was a tall, slender man with a full white beard who maintained the image of a serious college professor. His employees called him Dr. Loome because he had a doctorate in theology from the University of Tübingen in Germany.[3] While he was in Germany looking for books for his doctoral dissertation, Tom ran into the largest book dealer in Great Britain, Richard Booth of Hay-on-Wye in Wales. Booth was so impressed with his knowledge of rare theology books that he hired Tom to work for him. After getting his doctorate, Tom returned to the United States and taught theology at the College of St. Catherine in St. Paul, but he was more interested in the secondhand book business. In 1982 he opened his theology bookstore in the Old Swedish Covenant Church in Stillwater—right across the street from Jim Cummings's mansion—with the large stock of books he had accumulated over the years.

The Old Swedish Covenant Church, at 320 North Fourth Street, was built in 1904 by its congregation, Swedish laborers who had come to Stillwater to work in the sawmills. The church had unusual features, including a central auditorium with a floor that slanted toward the center, elaborate stained-glass windows, and a circular staircase. When Tom turned it into a bookstore, the bookcases had to be custom-built to accommodate the building's odd configurations.

He filled the church with theological books he bought from the many seminaries and libraries that were closing in the 1980s.[4] Where the average bookseller bought two hundred books at a time, Tom bought fifty thousand. These either went

[3] He studied under Joseph Ratzinger, who later became Pope Benedict XVI.

[4] Some excellent lieutenants managed Tom's operations, like Chris Lentz and Henry Stachyra, young men who shepherded many of the books Tom bought from theological institutions back to Stillwater.

Tom Loome at the Old Swedish Covenant Church in Stillwater.
Photograph by Brandi Jade Thomas/Pioneer Press.

into the church or were reconstituted into new libraries that Tom sold to other theological institutions. In eight years, from 1982 to 1990, this "bookstore in a church" became famous, and theologians, scholars, and librarians came from around the world to buy books there.

In 2018 the *Pioneer Press* recalled that "Loome became a national expert in rare books on theological subjects, hunting for treasures in university and college libraries and searching through private collections of deceased priests and ministers and in monasteries that had closed. At one point, Loome Theological Booksellers had the largest stock in North America of books on philosophy, theology, religion and related areas, including biblical exegesis and archaeology, ecclesiastical arts, patristic and medieval literature, liturgical texts and studies, religious biography and lives of the saints, canon law, and Protestant and Catholic Americana."

Once Tom decided to join us we rented the space at 216 Main, stripped the place bare, and lined the walls with bookcases. And we needed a lot of cases, because Tom and Jim were going to bring in a hundred thousand books: Tom had forty thousand general academic books in storage, and Jim had sixty thousand literary criticism and biography books at his house. I had the pitiable one thousand books left from the Arcade Street store that covered more lowbrow subjects, like hunting, fishing, children's, and baseball. We were equal partners, so even though I was only going to have a hundredth of the books in the store, I still paid a third of the expenses.[5]

I spent every dime of the money I'd gotten from Mike in the month and a half it took to put the store together. We filled it to the rafters with books, and I do mean rafters, because Jim insisted on ten-foot-high bookcases. The organization was pretty simple: we rented the space together, shared the expenses, and had our own books for sale; the books were coded with either a G, a C, or a T. We called the new store St. Croix Antiquarian Booksellers and stenciled the name on the window, in gold, with our three names beneath it.

From the day we opened, May 15, 1990, we had a steady stream of customers. Most said they had never been in a used bookstore before. You could see the wonder on their faces,

---

[5] The move to Stillwater and the expense of setting up the store didn't help my credit rating. Mary Pat and I were trying to figure out how to move to Stillwater from East St. Paul when, lo and behold, she found a house with an assumable VA mortgage. This meant we wouldn't have to qualify for a loan if we could come up with the down payment. We borrowed money from her father, and in July 1990 we moved to Stillwater with our five children. For those keeping track of the cars I drove, I had, at this time, a 1974 blue Vanagon, a huge vehicle with a tiny engine that drove like a pontoon. I bought it to haul books, but it was unwieldy, untrustworthy, and so underpowered it couldn't carry more than ten boxes without overheating.

Jim Cummings, Tom Loome, and Gary Goodman at 216 Main Street. Courtesy of Washington County Historical Society.

especially the middle-class suburban women and the business-men in suits and ties. Unaware of the six-hundred-year history of the secondhand book business, many asked, "What a great idea. Used books. Did you think of this?"

St. Croix Antiquarian entered the world as a first-class bookstore. Booksellers and collectors still had to travel to find books, so news of a new bookstore that included Tom Loome and Jim Cummings traveled fast. Surprisingly, I sold as many books as they did on the day we opened, and on most days thereafter. As I wrote many years later in a lighthearted tribute to Tom on his seventieth birthday: "I, fresh off selling my first bookstore in East St. Paul, had a mere 1,000 books. Luckily, I had the fields of low brow literature and inane pursuits to my-self and thus was able to hold my own. As Tom and Jim later learned, in the words of H. L. Mencken, no one ever went broke underestimating the intelligence of the American public."

We were only at 216 Main for a year. In March 1991, the owner of an appliance store a few doors down from us, at 232 South Main, died, and, partly as a favor to the local bankers who wanted the property off their books (the appliance guy had borrowed $500,000 against a building only worth $150,000), Jim decided to buy it. Tom and I weren't too happy about becoming Jim's tenants, but rent is rent, and it may as well be Jim collecting it.

The new location, my bookstore home for the next twenty-seven years, was twice the size of 216 and had been built in 1964 in the burned-out space of two previous buildings—a restaurant and a laundry—that had been demolished in 1942. (You can still see their charred outlines on the sides of the adjacent buildings.) Number 232 was one of downtown's newest buildings and of the most basic design: cinder block walls, a

Early St. Croix Antiquarian Booksellers
at 232 South Main Street, Stillwater.

steel and wooden beam ceiling, and a cement floor. When we moved in, it had a display area in the front and, further back, offices with fake walls covered in dark and uneven plywood paneling. From some stains on the floor you could tell the roof leaked. A smaller, separate back room was filled with mechanical parts from the 1940s and 1950s: manglers, wringers, and gasoline-powered dryer engines, all covered with an inch of dust.[6] A long, wide ramp led from the back door—great for hauling in books—and, below that, there was an industrial lift that still worked.

It took two months and several dumpsters just to get 232 cleared out.[7] We carpeted the front room and put in a wood floor and a rare book room. Then we moved five thousand boxes of books from 216 to 232 in an endless stream of hand carts wheeled from one store to the other. Soon after we opened, in May 1991, Jim decided he didn't want to be a landlord after all and offered to sell Tom and me a one-third interest in

---

[6] Pat Hicks, the first non–family member to work for me, later painted the concrete floor in the back room a bright red, an odd color choice for a young man who was, by all other measures, a sober and serious student. Pat was a great worker who studied Irish history and later became a professor at Augustana University in South Dakota. He has published several books of poetry and two critically acclaimed novels: *The Commandant of Lubizec,* about the Holocaust in World War II, and *In the Shadow of Dora,* about the Third Reich's V-2 rocket program.

[7] The first family member to work for me was my daughter Meghan, who started when she was twelve. The other five kids each started when they turned twelve too, and since I had six kids, at least one worked for me, without interruption, for almost twenty-five years. At first they straightened books and tidied up, but as they grew older they ran the store while I was away and managed my book search operations. Sure, there was some back talk and unreasonable demands, but I can say, without equivocation, without prejudice, that the hardest-working, best employees I ever had were my children.

the building. We jumped at the chance, not overly concerned that when Jim bought it, with the owner being dead and the bank anxious to move the property, the usual niceties of, say, a building inspection had been dispensed with. So of course, 232 turned out to not only be one of downtown's newest buildings but also one of the crappiest. What the builders had gained in space they made up for in cheap materials and questionable—some might say criminal—construction.

Once we were equal partners, the place developed a whole host of expensive physical problems. Most pressing was the leaky roof. Before the first year was out, we spent $30,000 on a new one. Next was the heating system, or lack thereof. The building was theoretically heated by an old boiler that generated steam for some pipes that ran along the ceiling and ended in mechanical fans. The fans, in turn, were supposed to blow warm air, but they were thirty years old and half didn't work, so in the winter the front of the store, which was only insulated from the cold by the two buildings on either side of it, topped out at a toasty fifty degrees. The back room had no protection whatsoever, so it was freezing—like frost-on-the-walls-type freezing. A new furnace and air conditioning unit cost us another $18,000, and even then the back room stayed pretty nippy in the winter.

We learned, too, about the seasonal nature of business in Stillwater. Tourists started coming at the end of May and business stayed strong until the end of October. The St. Croix River and the historical town brought in day-trippers who weren't afraid to spend money, but after the fall colors faded and the "leaf peepers" left, business dropped off a cliff. Tom, Jim, and I sold books through the mail, so this didn't affect us as much as the other businesses. So many small shops came and went that I called Main Street the street of broken dreams. Still, in less than two years, St. Croix Antiquarian Booksellers (usually called just St. Croix Books) became the most successful bookstore in Minnesota and possibly the Midwest. And during that time, I went from renting a duplex in East St. Paul to (sort of) owning a house and a third of a building in Stillwater, so things could have been worse.

9. Hoarding
and Horse Barns

*Luther posted his famous 95 theses in 1517; within three
years, his printed works had sold some 300,000 copies.
In Renaissance terms, this was the equivalent of cat videos.*
CULLEN MURPHY, The Atlantic, *January 2020*

ONCE I MOVED TO STILLWATER, I was able to buy books
in ways I never could on Arcade Street. People who were
moving or the relatives of someone who had died would call
the store with books to sell. This was a revelation. What, no
week on the road? No Danish dinners? You never knew what
you'd get from calls like these—it could be a pack rat's nightmare or a world-class collection of books.

One call I got was from the daughter of a University of Minnesota history professor who had died and left her a collection of books by and about Abraham Lincoln. She was sure
the books were valuable because her father had said one was
signed by Abraham Lincoln, a signature worth about $25,000
at the time. When I went through the books, I couldn't find
any that were signed, by Lincoln or anyone else, but I did find
some I could use, so I paid the daughter and assured her that if
I found the Lincoln signature, I would let her know.

As I was pricing the books back at the store, I noticed a small
pouch pasted in the back of the last volume of the common
Abraham Lincoln set by Carl Sandburg.[1] Inside was a pamphlet
published in 1864, and on the front, near the bottom, was what

---

[1] Lincoln forgeries have been a cottage industry almost from the day he
was assassinated, and even Sandburg was fooled by one fake. The frontis-
piece to the first volume of this set is a picture of an ax with Lincoln's "jack-

looked like Abraham Lincoln's signature. There was even a no-tarized statement from a man named William P. Brown, who claimed he had been Mary Todd Lincoln's coachman, that said, simply, "the signature is genuine." My son Nolan, who was in-terested in obscure pamphlets, was excited about this signature at first but did some research and then said, "I hate to break it to you, Pop, but I think that signature is a Coachman forgery."

The Coachman forgeries were a scheme dreamed up in the 1930s by Eugene "Pinny" Field II (the son of well-known poet and Chicago columnist Eugene Field)[2] and Harry Dayton Sick-les. Sickles was a marginal dealer who sold rare books directly to buyers from hotel rooms or, in a pinch, from the trunk of his car. The two criminals hooked up when Eugene Sr. died and the prodigal son, Pinny—so nicknamed because his parents dressed him up in pinafores when he was little—returned to Chicago to settle the estate. Once there, he immediately began selling off parts of his famous father's library. In his 2001 book *Absolutely, Mr. Sickles? Positively, Mr. Field!,* William Butts de-scribes how the Coachman scheme evolved:

> After Pinny's supply of genuine material from his fa-ther's library ran out, he and Sickles turned to some un-derhanded tricks to make common merchandise more

---

knife signature" carved into the handle. This was miraculously discovered in perfect condition buried in New Salem, Illinois, in the 1930s—one hundred years after Abe supposedly used it—and accepted as genuine for many years.

[2] Field wrote children's poems, such as "Wynken, Blynken, and Nod." He also wrote "The Bibliomaniac's Prayer":

> So banish from my erring heart
> All baleful appetites and hints
> Of Satan's fascinating art,
> Of first editions, and of prints.
> Direct me in some godly walk
> Which leads away from bookish strife.

desirable. They forged signatures of the elder Field and other famous individuals on mundane items to make them attractive to prospective buyers. These forgeries, filtered through Pinny Field, offering the implication that the book or pamphlet originated in the famous library of Eugene Field, fooled more than one collector.

The most famous forgeries produced by Sickles and Field are known as the "Coachman Forgeries." They stem from a national news story in 1931 that reported that a man named William P. Brown claimed to have served as a coachman for Mary Todd Lincoln during the years following her husband's assassination. Sickles and Field developed a scheme whereby they could use Brown's moment of fame to lend a note of credibility to their forgeries. The two con artists gathered together a number of period books, pamphlets, and maps for Brown to sign.

So, after Brown signed the items and had his signature notarized, Sickles and Field added the forged autographs. Besides Eugene Field and Abraham Lincoln, they produced forgeries of Bret Harte, Rudyard Kipling, Theodore Roosevelt, and Mark Twain.

The Coachman forgeries became minor collector's items in their own right, and I sold the Lincoln pamphlet for $500, a far cry from the $25,000 I had hoped for. It took some doing, though, to convince the Lincoln collector's daughter that the signature her father had treasured all his life was, in fact, a forgery.

The earliest printed book I ever handled came from a woman who brought in some of her late brother's books. One was a version of a Roman Missal, called the *Missale Leodiensis,* printed in 1502. This was so old that at first I didn't know what it was. It was big—bigger than most old bibles—and had wooden covers. The interior was in very good condition, but the covers were battered and the back strip (spine) was missing. There was no title or copyright page. It just began with a Latin text beautifully printed in red and black letters.

When I first looked at it, I told the lady that without a title page, the book, despite its beauty, would be hard to sell because there was no way to determine its age, but she was in a hurry and just wanted to get rid of this and the rest of her brother's books. I later discovered that it was published before title pages—first introduced in 1501—were widely used and that the title, date, and place of publication were in the back in, by the way, old-style, hard-to-read Latin. I have handled pages from the *Nuremberg Chronicle,* printed in 1493, fragments of books printed in the 1470s and 1480s, and pages handwritten on vellum from the thirteenth and fourteenth centuries, but the *Missale* was the earliest intact printed book I ever came across.

I also found out that this was one of only four known copies of the *Missale Leodiensis* in existence, and an unusual variant at that. There were several versions of the Roman Missal before 1570, but at the Council of Trent that year, Pope Pius V decreed that only one version—the *Missale Romanum*—would be sanctioned by the church. Earlier versions like the *Missale Leodiensis* were "blasphemies" and to be burned. This was one that escaped the hell fires. A fascinating feature of the book was two pages of handwritten Latin text of Gospel and Bible passages accompanied by whimsical drawings, like a chicken, birds flying, and a caricature of a guy with a beard. Someone in 1502, it seemed, had too much time on his (not likely her) hands.

———————

The oddest place I ever went to buy books was a horse barn. One winter, the owner of a horse boarding business called and said that her caretaker—a man who had worked for her for over twenty years—had dropped dead of a heart attack while washing a load of horse blankets. The caretaker had lived in a small apartment up two flights of stairs in the barn above a large, enclosed exercise area surrounded by a wooden walkway. The owner hadn't been in this guy's apartment since she hired him, so imagine her surprise when she opened his door and found three thousand books on Freemasonry, the occult, and mysticism.

When I got there, the only furniture in the apartment was a bed and a lounge chair in front of a small TV. The rest of the place was filled with books, including in the kitchen, bedroom, and bathroom. I could tell this guy was a serious collector—he bought his books through the mail and paid plenty for the scarcer titles. A portion of the collection was on occult fraternal organizations, like the Freemasons, Odd Fellows, Rosicrucians, and Knights Templar. Another batch was on the Theosophical Society, founded in 1875 to study the occult, Eastern religions, and the Kabbalah. A bookseller could retire in splendor with a constant supply of early books on Freemasonry and the occult, so I bought them from the caretaker's nephew, who showed up later.

Now it was a matter of getting them out of an unheated horse barn, in the dead of a Minnesota winter, down two flights of slippery wooden stairs. The books were in decent condition, but a thin layer of horsehair and horse dust (the composition of which I will leave to the reader's imagination) covered everything in the apartment.

The caretaker also had a thing for strong-smelling incense, so the place smelled like a Buddhist temple would smell if Buddhist temples kept horses. The apartment was hot, there was barely room to move, and the front door opened directly onto the walkway, where the temperature was about ten degrees below zero.

There are times when being the son of a poor bookseller is a fate worse than death, and I'm sure that's how Nolan felt when I drafted him to help me move those books. It took us a full day, from the morning into the night, sweating, freezing, covered in horsehair and horse dust. We nearly broke our necks navigating the stairs that led to the apartment. I don't remember what I paid Nolan for that job, but whatever it was, it wasn't enough.

The most out-of-the-way place I ever went to buy books was in Alaska, where in the summer of 1995 I went to fish for salmon with my friend Mark Ziegler. At a bookstore in Anchorage I heard that a retired couple from England had shipped over several thousand books to a former Russian settlement called Seldovia—a small town with a population of less than three hundred people—and opened a used bookstore. It was so remote that the only way to get there was by plane or boat.

A trove of untouched books like that is like catnip for a bookseller, so I went to the Homer airport and bought a forty-dollar plane ticket to Seldovia, a twelve-minute flight over a small part of the Cook Inlet. The wind was howling. When the flight was called, I was directed to a small, very old propeller plane where the pilot—who looked hungover and like he had just come into town after a month out in the bush—was holding the plane down with a couple of ropes. He told me we were lucky: the wind was right at forty miles an hour—any higher and the flight would have been canceled. I have to say, without exaggerating, that flight might have been the scariest twelve minutes of my life.

Once we got into the air the wind was so strong the pilot had to "crab" the plane—fly it at a forty-five-degree angle. Then the plane would regularly, and abruptly, drop about forty feet. I sat in the back (the plane only had four seats) with an older Native Alaskan woman who was knitting some sort of cap and didn't seem to notice anything out of the ordinary. After one wicked drop, the pilot turned to me and said, "So, where are you from?" like this was just another ho-hum flight. He was eating a Snickers and drinking a Coke, items I only remember because I thought they would be the last things I'd see before I died. Obviously, we made it to Seldovia, but once we got there, they had to tie the plane down so it wouldn't blow away.

Seldovia was built on the mud flats along the edge of the Cook Inlet. The summer I was there the buildings in town were on stilts and the visiting tourists walked on wooden pathways that could be pulled up and stored away in the winter. One of the more popular stores in town sold seal-blubber fudge and jars of pickled fish. There was a wooden Russian Orthodox church in the center of town that had a gift shop that sold religious items, like crosses and icons, and near the church, in this small fishing village in the middle of nowhere, was a genuine used bookstore. The British couple that started it just thought Seldovia would be a good place to retire and sell secondhand books. Hard to argue with that, especially if you like pickled fish. I bought $400 worth of books from them but was so scared of flying back to Homer I took the ferry.

The most depressing place I ever went to buy books came from a call I got from the wife of a bookseller who lived in San Diego. Her husband, Joe, had developed dementia and she wondered if I'd be interested in buying several thousand books that he had left over from his bookselling days. From quotes

I had gotten from Joe, I knew they'd be good, but I'd have to figure out how to buy a batch of books larger and farther away than any I'd handled before. Jim and Tom could tell me how to ship them back to Minnesota, but getting the money to buy them was another story. For this, Jim introduced me to Dave Pohl, a banker at a family-owned bank in Stillwater. Dave, Jim said, wasn't big on paperwork or credit checks and would lend you money if he thought you'd pay it back. Well, of course, I told Dave, I'll pay the money back. Just tell me where to sign.

Once I secured the financing, I flew to San Diego and met Joe, a man in his early sixties in the later stages of dementia, and his wife, Carol, a very dignified, put-together woman. Joe was short, Italian, curly haired, with a dark complexion. He was cheerful and playful around his daughters, who constantly wandered in and out of the house, but became perplexed and agitated whenever Carol asked him a question or told him to do something. Joe was aware enough to know that I was there for a nefarious purpose—to take his books—so he watched every move I made. He would not talk to me, and if I shifted something or talked to Carol about the books, he would scream and run from the room. Carol told me she was going to put him in a nursing home.

They lived in a large, distinguished house with a pool and a backyard full of orange and olive trees. Carol said Joe was a very successful bookseller in his day, but I wondered how they could afford that house based on what booksellers usually make. I got the impression there might have been some inherited money involved. Joe had closed his San Diego store ten years earlier and kept his leftover books, the books he quoted to other booksellers, in a shed behind his house. Walking into it was like walking into a time capsule. His better books— illustrated children's, signed sporting, hunting, and fishing, and leather-bound books—were in the house itself.[3] Carol told me how much she wanted for the books and said I couldn't pick and choose: if I wanted them, I had to take them all. As it turned out, I would have offered five times what she asked, but the money didn't seem to matter to her. She just wanted to get rid of the books. I suggested that we could leave some for Joe, so he wouldn't be so upset, but Carol said no: he wasn't going to need any books where he was going.

While I packed up, Joe would sneak books from the boxes and run away and Carol would scold him like a child. This went on for the better part of three days. The look-alike daughters would walk through, pet their distraught father, and glare at me like I was the devil incarnate. I understood how they felt. Joe had already lost much of his identity, and I was, in a sense, taking away the last remnants. I felt bad for him, and I hoped his dementia made him forget that I was buying his books.

Finding good books on house calls, though, was the exception rather than the rule. One call I got was from some grown children who wanted to sell their dead father's collection of 250,000 paperbacks. (If the average paperback weighs a quarter of a pound, that's thirty-one tons of books.) The books were in a ramshackle house in a run-down neighborhood. To save space, the father had built an elaborate system of shelving—like a library system—where the cases had to be rolled out to get at the books. These ingeniously constructed cases were everywhere: in the kitchen, the bathrooms, the basement, and the garage. When I got to the house, the dead man's widow was in

[3] Some of the leather-bound books were signed bindings, in which the binder has stamped their name or initials in small letters on the book's inner cover. I kept some of these myself and started a collection that I added to for more than thirty years.

the kitchen in her nightgown smoking a cigarette. She probably hadn't cooked a meal in that kitchen in twenty years.

This man collected paperbacks of different titles and every edition of that title. So if he had an early Pocket Book of, say, *The Mystery on the Golf Course,* he also had all the later editions and any edition published in a foreign language. The time, money, and effort it took to do this was unimaginable. I could see a scholar collecting first editions of hardcover copies of an important book, but for paperback mysteries and popular fiction, it was just unreal.

The children had high hopes for this, their inheritance. They wanted two dollars each for the paperbacks—a half a million dollars. I had to break it to them that with the exception of some early, collectible items, the books were worthless. Not only that but getting rid of them would cost thousands of dollars. They might even have to tear down the house to do it. I'm sure they called other dealers for another opinion, but nobody in their right mind was going to touch that paperback house of horrors.

As long as we're on the subject of people who go overboard when it comes to accumulating books, I should mention Raylene, one of the more colorful "collectors" in St. Paul. Her lifelong quest was to find twelve family albums her mother had sold at a sale when Raylene was a young girl. She obsessively hunted for those albums at garage sales, estate sales, and bookstores and, remarkably, found a few over the years. But she also found other books; so many, in fact, that she completely filled three houses in the Midway district of St. Paul—houses the city sold for a dollar to people who would fix them up—with books. After she died, they discovered that one of the houses was so structurally compromised from the weight of the books that it had to be torn down.

Then there is Madeline Kripke, who crammed the world's largest known collection of dictionaries into her small Greenwich Village apartment. The only furniture in the apartment was a lounge chair, a bed, and a working stove. Everything else, from floor to ceiling, was books. (She was nearly evicted in the 1990s because of them.) "Beginning with the Webster's Collegiate that her parents gave her in the fifth grade, she accumulated an estimated 20,000 volumes as diverse as a Latin dictionary printed in 1502, Jonathan Swift's 1722 booklet titled *The Benefits of Farting Explained,* and the New York Metropolitan Transportation Authority's 1980 guide to pickpocket slang," wrote Sam Roberts in the *New York Times.* It was an astounding collection, revered by lexicographers, but rendered obsolete by the internet. No one knew what would happen to it when Kripke died from COVID-19 in April 2020.

Another case of excessive book collecting involved the Collyer brothers, Homer and Langley, who died in 1947 in a brownstone at 2078 Fifth Avenue in New York that they had inherited from their parents. After some neighbors complained about a terrible smell, the brothers' bodies were found under 140 tons of junk, including thousands of books. In *Book Row,* Marvin Mondlin and Roy Meador detail how the Wavrovics brothers, New York booksellers, bought the mansion on the condition that they dispose of everything in it. Afterward, they refused to discuss what they found there, but people got the impression it wasn't exactly the deal of the century.

10. *Travels to Book Towns*

Who so would be a man
must be a nonconformist.

RALPH WALDO EMERSON, *"Self-Reliance"*

S T. CROIX BOOKS attracted booksellers and collectors from
all over the world. Alan Page, Garrison Keillor, and Jonathan Winters came in; Sam Shepard and Jessica Lange, who
lived in Stillwater, were regulars. So was the poet Robert Bly,
another Minnesotan. As Mike Frain, who worked for me for
twenty years, described it, "There were scores of people over
the years from all over the world who were incredible in count-
less ways. There were actual Arctic explorers, noted authors,
major military people, scholars, New Age weirdos. One day, I
had a very colorful guy in who claimed to have been a major
force and experimenter of LSD in the early '60s in California."
Other regular customers were David Mech, the famous wolf re-
searcher; William Least Heat-Moon, aka William Trogdon, the
Osage travel writer; Ann Bancroft, the first woman to complete
expeditions to the Arctic and Antarctic; and Dr. W. Bruce Fye,
a medical historian and author of several books on the history
of medicine. Fye was, by the way, a used book dealer himself.

Larry McMurtry, the novelist who wrote books set in the
West, including *The Last Picture Show* and *Lonesome Dove,*
was a customer. He also happened to be one of the largest secondhand book dealers in the country. He had created his own
"book town" in Archer City, Texas—the small town where he
was born—by buying several buildings in the town's deserted

business district and turning them into bookstores. [1] He wanted
to turn Archer City into a Hay-on-Wye, the town full of bookstores in Wales started by the British bookseller Richard Booth.
Later, Stillwater got on the book town bandwagon, so it will be
instructive, in this and the next chapter, to describe the trips I
took to Archer City and Hay-on-Wye to see the impact so many
used bookstores had on these two very different towns.

First, something about Larry McMurtry's background as
a bookseller. It began in the mid-1960s, when he worked as a
book scout while he was a student at Rice University in Houston. After that he was hired by the wealthy David family—
Henry and Grace—to run the Bookman, a store that the
couple's son, Dorman David, started with a $1.5 million in-
heritance he got from his grandfather. (Grace David was the
inspiration for the character Aurora Greenway in McMurtry's
novel *Terms of Endearment*.)

After he bought the building for the Bookman, Dorman David stocked it with rare western Americana, western art, and
Texas history books that he purchased from other dealers, often at exorbitant prices. As McMurtry describes in his 2009
memoir, "With his building in hand, all Dorman needed was
stock. Undaunted, but with much of his million and a half gone,
Dorman set off on a tour of the major dealers in Texana and

---

[1] Before the 1990s, the closest thing to a book town might have been the
well-known cluster of twenty or so bookshops called Book Row on Fourth
Avenue in New York City from the 1890s to the 1960s. Collectively, the
stores carried nearly two million used books, and, as Travis McDade notes in
Thieves of Book Row, the area "was the one place where book buyers would
travel in search of books, knowing that if one of a dozen shops did not have
a particular item, it might be found in another." In his *Adventures in American Bookshops, Antique Stores and Auction Rooms*, written in 1922, Guido
Bruno notes, "no matter how large and complete the stock of a secondhand
bookseller might be, his neighbor's collection will be quite different." Con-
centrations of bookstores attracted attention, and not much in the secondhand book world at that time generated as much publicity as a book town.

Americana generally. He went to the Eberstadts, then the deans of the Americanists. He went to Lathrop Harper. He went east and he went west, buying choice items but at stiff prices. In general, the major dealers were intrigued with Dorman, but not so intrigued that they forgot how to work the cash register. Here was a young man who made selling fun."

According to Gregory Curtis of *Texas Monthly*, the Bookman "was a place of such stunning grandeur that it actually worked against the success of Dorman's business. Customers who wandered in were often too intimidated to buy. Unfortunately, his personal confusion and flaws of character overwhelmed even his perfect taste. He became a heroin addict. He was indicted for receiving stolen books. He was suspected to be the mastermind behind a ring of thieves who looted libraries and archives across Texas." As noted in the earlier section on John Jenkins in chapter 4, David was also the one bookseller who admitted he had a hand in forging the Texas Declarations of Independence that led to Jenkins's undoing.

David's forgeries were so well done that they fooled every dealer, librarian, and collector who examined them. They went undetected until Tom Taylor, the author of *Texfake*, became suspicious of the number of Texas Declarations of Independence coming onto the market. This was all the more remarkable because David made the fake documents while he was deep into a heroin addiction. "Old friends who might stop by would see him in the bathroom with a needle in his arm," Curtis wrote. "Others would come in to find him sitting loopy-eyed in front of the television. He missed enough business appointments that even loyal associates finally gave up on him. In the midst of all this David did nothing to hide his fakes." Despite David's shortcomings, "nearly every woman who ever met him fell in love with him," John Jenkins said. "He got married six times and had so many girlfriends he couldn't keep them straight."

Once his inheritance was gone, David borrowed money from loan sharks to cover his day-to-day expenses, and when he couldn't pay the money back, the sharks threatened to kill him. To raise funds, he put his rarest books up for auction, but this didn't cover his debts, so he fled to Mexico on extended *vacaciones*. While Dorman was on the lam, his mother, Grace, decided she and an elderly socialite friend were going to run the Bookman. As they were sorting through the mess Dorman left, Larry McMurtry wandered in and suggested a solution—they should hire him to run the store. "As a commercial venture the Bookman was hopeless from the first," McMurtry recalls in his memoir. "At one point, Grace had a penthouse built onto the property—the penthouse contained a wall-sized aquarium, containing hundreds of lovely, mysterious fish. What it cost to maintain I never knew."

McMurtry worked for the David family for three years, until Dorman, back from Mexico, showed up with some rare Texas historical documents: "letters from Sam Houston, Stephen F. Austin, and the like, most of them addressed to the commandant of the port of Galveston. These documents were of the first importance, dealing, as they did, with the Texans' efforts to free themselves from Mexico." Some of the documents—not a surprise where Dorman was concerned—had been stolen from the Rosenberg Library in Galveston. When McMurtry thought the David family might try to sell them, he decided to leave the Bookman. (McMurtry believed some of this material later made its way to John Jenkins.)

In 1970, McMurtry moved to the Georgetown area in Washington, DC, and with a couple of partners opened Booked Up, a store he owned for eighteen years. Rising real estate prices forced him out of Georgetown, so he moved Booked Up to his hometown of Archer City—the setting for his third novel, *The Last Picture Show*—and bought several vacant buildings in the abandoned downtown. He filled them with a half a million books he bought from the many old, established secondhand bookstores closing in the late '80s and early '90s.

A 2013 article by Paul Knight in *Texas Monthly* describes McMurtry's operation:

> His books, a handpicked collection sold out of four stores he named Booked Up, defined Archer City for decades. McMurtry opened the first shop in 1987, at a time when his fame soared from the success of *Lonesome Dove* and Archer City reeled from the collapse of oil prices. During the next ten years, McMurtry bought up vacant storefronts on the square and filled them with hundreds of thousands of books. He dreamed of creating a book town, not unlike Hay-on-Wye, a village in Wales that started with one store and eventually attracted dozens of booksellers. He took out ads in bibliophile magazines. "Miraculous birth!" they read. "Visit the newly born book town of Archer City, Texas, and help the endless migration of good books continue." A shuttered hotel was renovated and reopened, and the town's original hospital was turned into a bed and breakfast, both to accommodate the carloads of buyers and McMurtry fans who made the long journey to Archer City.

I stopped in Archer City in 1993 on my way to San Antonio, where I was going to look at a collection of books a quoter wanted to sell (more on that in a moment). Archer City is in the middle of nowhere, a long detour on the way to Dallas across the flat and windy North Texas plains. When I got to the town it was deserted. A few cars were parked in front of a local café, but there weren't any retail businesses besides McMurtry's four bookstores—each named with a number, as in Booked Up No. 1, Booked Up No. 2, and so forth. No hardware stores, antique shops, or grocery stores. Archer City, as the author Susan Sontag once said, was Larry McMurtry's own theme park.

McMurtry lived in a three-story house in town, a few doors down from the single-story house where he grew up and not far from the high school where he graduated as part of a senior class of nineteen in 1954. *The Last Picture Show* is set in a town like Archer City, where a wealthy local businessman gives two high school boys a pool hall and a movie theater to entice them to put down roots in their small Texas town. The movie theater described in the book is still there; the back is gutted, but the front has been restored to look like it did in the 1950s, when the events in the book take place. A movie based on the book was filmed almost entirely in Archer City and features appearances by a very young Cybill Shepherd, Jeff Bridges, and Randy Quaid.

I called ahead, and Larry made a point of being at the store when I arrived, a sign of his usual hospitality to other booksellers. He was a quiet, almost shy man, stocky, with a wary look and a wry sense of humor. He came across as a regular guy, not self-important at all, more interested in books and bookselling than anything else. As you entered the flagship store, Booked Up No. 1, the front room was filled with rare books any store in the country would have been proud to own; in the rest of that store and in the other three buildings, large spaces were given over to specific subjects—like the rooms in Melvin McCosh's mansion—so half a building might be American history and the other half fiction.

Unlike Melvin and his run-down house, though, McMurtry spared no expense in design or decoration. There were Native American and western artifacts all over, beadwork and buffalo skulls, that looked like they belonged in a museum. The bookcases and other fixtures were perfectly constructed. When I walked in, McMurtry was pricing a bunch of books about cats at a back counter—hundreds of older cat books that I'd never seen before, many published in England, so I bought a bunch. I sold some over the years but still had plenty left twenty years later. (I've always said that you can't go wrong buying books about snakes, but, as a general rule, stay away from cat books.)

McMurtry's stores contained the stock of over twenty-six extinct secondhand bookstores, including the Gotham Book Mart in New York, Leary's in Philadelphia, Heritage Book Shop in Beverly Hills, and Goodspeed's Book Shop in Boston. Larry collected their signs and displayed them as a reminder of a bygone era. He would tell the story of the first secondhand bookstore he ever went to, when he was in high school—Barbara's Bookstore in Ft. Worth, Texas, where he bought a novel by Hugh Walpole. Forty years later, when he went back and bought the store's entire stock, many of the same books he had seen when he bought the Walpole novel were still there.

McMurtry reflected on the state of the secondhand book business in an August 30, 2011, article in the *New Yorker* by James McAuley. "It's tragic," he said. "It's just clear that bookselling as it's been basically since Gutenberg—a form of dispensing culture, if you will—is clearly passing away. I don't think we have a reading culture anymore. Five years ago, I would have thought I was leaving my son and my grandson a great asset, and now I'm not sure I am."

In a weeklong auction in 2012 that he called the Last Book Sale, McMurtry sold off half of his stock. (One couple bought several thousand books and planned on opening a store that featured "free same-day bike delivery of used books.") An article by Michael Agresta about the sale in *The Atlantic* noted:

> Much of Booked Up's stock was effectively worthless, based on online valuation at least, and McMurtry's approach of mixing rare books and shelf-filler into large auction lots meant that most buyers were returning

home with a lot of dead weight, commercially speaking. Flatlining demand for printed books and growing online markets for rare books have pushed many dealers out of retail spaces and onto the Internet. There, dealers have no need for browsing stock and can concentrate on a small stable of very valuable books of interest to serious collectors. The interesting but easily attainable books that made up much of Booked Up's stock will continue to decline in value.

McMurtry's book town was hurt by the internet, like the rest of the book business, and by its out-of-the-way location. As of 2020 a couple of stores still managed to limp along, and the website proclaimed, "To All Book People: Rumors that we have moved or been sold are pernicious nonsense! We are right where we have been for so long—on Main St. in Archer City." Despite the time and money McMurtry spent trying to make Archer City a book town, his stores were all that was there. Stillwater and Hay-on-Wye were both, at least, located on rivers, in picturesque surroundings, with other shops and restaurants nearby. All Archer City had was high winds in the winter, oppressive heat in the summer, and a deserted downtown. People like the *idea* of books and bookstores, but when it gets above a hundred on the Texas prairie and the blue flies are buzzing, not many casual book buyers are going to drive a hundred miles out of their way to go to a place like Archer City. Larry, novelist, screenwriter, and, above all, bookseller, died on March 26, 2021, at the age of eighty-four.

After I left Archer City, I drove the 350 miles to San Antonio to look at the books that the abovementioned quoter wanted to sell. This is a grim ride: a barren landscape of rabid preachers on the radio, scattered Jesus posters, barbecue joints, taco stands, gun shops, and beat-up gas stations, their signs sand-blasted pale by the relentless winds. When I got to San Antonio—an oasis on the San Antonio River—and saw the books, they looked more like the leftover stock from a bookstore than something a collector would put together. Still, there were some good ones there, especially western Americana and fur trade stuff, which at the time sold well. The quoter, named Gerald, said he had to sell the books because he had a terminal heart condition and only a year to live. He was asking $15,000, and, considering the circumstances, I didn't haggle even though I only wanted, and only planned on taking, about a third of the books. When I talked to Tom, though, he suggested I take them all because, he said, "You can unload them on Richard Booth when he comes to Stillwater." I decided to do this but later came to regret it.

Gerald and his father, Chuck, lived in a cool, dark, and sparsely furnished hacienda-style house in the suburbs of San Antonio. Before he got sick Gerald had been a computer programmer, but his company went bankrupt and he lost his health insurance—hence the book sale. With all the bad news, the house was a pretty somber place. The one bright spot was Chuck, a former actor and director in his later sixties who believed he still could make a blockbuster movie. (He even offered me, in the strictest confidence, the once-in-a-lifetime opportunity of becoming an investor.) From some muttered comments, I deduced that Gerald had invested in this blockbuster—a "sure thing" according to Chuck—and hadn't been paid back.

The movie, or the preparations for a movie, was called *Shark Man*, about a man who becomes a mutant after being (surprise!) doused with radiation. The Shark Man could change to a half man, half shark, either top or bottom, at will. There were posters, props, and promotional materials about this movie all over the house: key chains, matchbooks, sun visors, a plaster cast of a half man and half shark, a statue of a man with a shark's head with a baby seal in its mouth. One poster was like the one for *Jaws,* only this one showed the shark man (bottom shark this time, but with big shark teeth) coming from beneath the water toward a scantily clad woman on a surfboard. Chuck said he wasn't sure if the shark man was a hero or villain, something the woman on the surfboard would have liked to know and something you might want to nail down before spending your dying son's money on posters and key chains.

I only had three days to organize packing and shipping the fifteen thousand books to Minnesota. (That's about seven hundred boxes, or fourteen tons, of books; they would fill the better part of a semitrailer.) Chuck was willing to help and, being a former movie director, turned out to be an organizational wizard. He picked up several Spanish-speaking workers from a group that gathered in the San Antonio warehouse district every morning and set up an assembly-line packing operation in the back yard of the hacienda. The workers called me *jefe* and handled the books with such reverence that I told them—or had Chuck tell them, since I didn't speak Spanish—not to be so careful or the job would take a month. The books made it safely to Minnesota a couple of weeks later. There were so many I didn't want (the books Tom suggested I take) that I had to rent a warehouse outside of town, hoping I could sell them to Richard Booth when he came to Stillwater.

11. The King
of Hay-on-Wye

*The enormous multiplication of
books in every branch of knowledge
is one of the greatest evils of this age.*
EDGAR ALLAN POE, *1842*

I WENT TO THE OTHER BOOK TOWN, Hay-on-Wye in Wales,
in the fall of 1993, a trip I was encouraged to take by Tom
Loome, who loved buying books in England and used Hay-on-
Wye as his base of operations. This was the small town full of
bookstores created by Richard Booth, Tom's friend and former
employer. Booth was the best known, and by all accounts the
most eccentric, bookseller in the United Kingdom. He was born
in Plymouth, England, in 1939 to Philip Booth, an army officer,
and Elizabeth Pitt, an heir to the Yardley soapmaking family.
His family moved to Hay-on-Wye—commonly called Hay—in
Wales when Richard was a boy, but he left to go to school at
Rugby and Oxford. When his uncle, Major Willie Booth, died
in 1961 and left him the family estate, called Brynmelyn, Richard moved back to Hay.

When Booth returned, the rural town of Hay was in economic decline, so property was cheap. With not much else to
do, and because books were a long-standing interest of his, he
bought a burned-out fire station and turned it into a secondhand bookstore.[1] When he discovered that libraries across the

---

[1] For those who like odd coincidences, Melvin McCosh also had a bookstore in a burned-out fire station.

United Kingdom were cleaning out their shelves and dumping thousands of books, Booth bought other buildings in Hay and filled them with the discards. By the late 1960s, his stores attracted book-buying students and counterculture radicals from the Bristol, Birmingham, Oxford, and Aberystwyth universities. The stores also attracted tourists, which caused other booksellers to move to Hay. By the mid-1970s there were over thirty bookstores in town, and Hay became known internationally as the Town of Books.

One building Booth bought for next to nothing was Hay Castle, a medieval fortification built around 1200 that played an important part in Welsh history, if only for the number of times it changed hands. It was attacked and ransacked during the First and Second Barons' Wars, the wars with the Welsh princes, the rebellion of Owain Glyndwr, and the Wars of the Roses. In the 1600s a separate mansion was built alongside the castle towers and the property turned into a private home. Major fires in both 1939 and 1977 destroyed the structures' interiors, but the castle itself survived. During the 1977

Hay-on-Wye, Wales. Photograph by Andy Scott. Creative Commons CC-BY-SA 4.0.

Hay Castle and the Honesty Bookshop.

fire Booth was asleep inside the castle and said he thought the sound from the crackling flames was his loyal subjects cheering for him. He filled bookcases along the outer walls of the castle with discarded, beat-up books that he called the Honesty Bookshop, where people paid for any books that they took on the honor system. (Booth claimed people were too honest. He said he made more money on the cheap books than he did on the books in the store.) In the 1960s he also held raucous parties at the castle, with guests that included the Rolling Stones and Marianne Faithfull.[2]

---

[2] Faithfull was a pop singer who occasionally hid out in Hay in the 1960s because the London police thought she was selling LSD to other celebrities. From the August 22, 1983, issue of *People* magazine: "To be sure, the locals have looked askance at some of Booth's friends—notably Marianne Faithfull, the ex-consort of Mick Jagger, and April Ashley, the striking blonde who, until her sex change operation a few years back, was a sailor in the merchant marine."

After a run-in with the Wales Tourist Board in 1977, Booth declared Hay an independent nation and appointed himself king. And why not? He already had a castle. This generated enormous publicity. Six television stations came to Hay to listen to him explain why the town was no longer part of the United Kingdom. According to the *Independent*'s Cole Moreton, "The Hay Air Force—a bi-plane—made a fly-past, a rowing boat was launched as the Hay Navy, and the sovereign retired to the pub to name his government. It was April Fools' Day, and the King was wearing a crown made out of tinfoil. The orb and scepter were made from the contents of a toilet."

King Richard issued passports and printed money for the Kingdom of Hay. He appointed a Hay House of Lords and installed his horse as the prime minister. For years, Booth would confer a title—duke, duchess, earl, countess, baron, baroness, knight, or lady—for a modest fee. He held cabinet meetings for the kingdom monthly at a local pub, and topics were chosen by spinning a game show–type wheel that had spaces like "have a drink," "defer to next session," and "chop off her head." Booth also ran a local intelligence agency, called the CI Hay, and rewarded whoever brought him the juiciest bits of gossip with a royal title and a pint of Guinness. The success of Hay helped him launch his next act, which was to promote the concept of book towns around the world as a way to revive rural communities.

For my first trip to Hay, I had planned to buy books like I did in the United States: I'd fly in, rent a car, go to local bookstores, and stay in hotels along the way. But traveling in England then, alone, on business, without GPS, was like being in a cold, damp hell. It was cold and rainy when I got there, cold and rainy when I left, and cold and rainy every day in between. The car I rented had a manual transmission, with the steering wheel and clutch on the U.S. passenger side, and, of course, the cars drove on the opposite side of the road. The roundabouts, odd (to me) signage, and lack of street signs—the street names, if there were any at all, were on the sides of buildings—made getting around a nightmare. Asking for directions didn't help, since they usually included something like "take a left at Barstow's sheep barn."

The food also seemed uniformly weird to me: half-cooked bacon, anemic-looking vegetables, gummy cheese, and meat pies made from leftover gizzards, hearts, livers, and, that finest of delicacies, intestines. The fish in the classic fish and chips was so greasy you got heart palpitations just looking at it. The temperature inside the cramped bed-and-breakfasts I stayed at was about sixty degrees and the bathwater even colder. The food and accommodations have gotten better in the last twenty years but can still be pretty grim if you rub elbows, as I did, with the lower classes.

I was lost most of the time. There were no roadside restaurants or hotel chains like there are today, so if you needed a place to stay or something to eat you had to go into a town. On my first night, at around ten p.m., I drove into Reading, a town about two hours west of London. Since I hadn't slept for twenty-four hours and was desperate for a place to stay, I stopped at an open pub where, inside, a bunch of soccer hooligans were playing darts. I asked the proprietor if he knew where I could find a room and he said, "Why, of course I do. We have a couple of rooms right here. And they come with a full English breakfast." The price for the room and breakfast was ten pounds—about sixteen dollars U.S.—which, even in 1993, was one step above a cardboard box on skid row.

I figured it would be bad, but I took it anyway. The bed was a thick piece of foam rubber covered with a sheet. The bathroom, down the hall, had a large grate that covered half the floor, and through it you could clearly see and hear the hooligans playing darts in the bar below. They, in turn, looked up expectantly whenever they heard a noise from the loo. The place smelled like beans and bangers, fish and chips, and, I thought, boiled intestines—my nose not yet finely tuned enough to make that distinction. Still, the sheet (singular) seemed clean enough, and I was so tired I lay down and slept until morning. When I left, the proprietor asked me how I wanted my English breakfast—with or without stewed tomatoes—and I told him that I regretfully would not be dining with them that morning. If the breakfast was anything like the room, I probably saved myself a case of botulism.

I wandered around England for a few days, lost and cold, subsisting on cheese baguettes and anemic tomatoes, before finally making it to Hay. I was supposed to have dinner with Richard Booth in the evening, so I spent the afternoon looking around the town. Hay is a classically beautiful English town located in the craggy, wild area of the Black Mountains of Wales on the River Wye. Two Norman castles and their fortifications—including Richard's own Hay Castle—are still there. The town was, indeed, full of books. There were two or three bookstores on every block. The largest was the Hay Cinema Bookshop, which, as the name implies, was in an old theater. This huge store was one of four, including the one in the castle, that Richard owned.

My dinner with Richard was going to be at Brynmelyn, the manor on his ancestral estate that had, like Melvin McCosh's mansion on Lake Minnetonka, about forty rooms. It was in better condition than Melvin's place but still quite seedy. As I recall, the large wooden front doors had stained-glass windows on either side with dramatic portrayals of Richard as the king of Hay; one I remember showed him dressed as a knight slaying a dragon. When I knocked on the door, a servant wearing a garage mechanic–type jumpsuit answered and said, "Ah, Mr. Goodman. Richard is expecting you."

The servant ushered me through what I supposed was the great hall. High up, lining the walls, were hunting trophies: two-thirds were deer heads with racks of antlers, but there were also more exotic animals, maybe a tiger and a water buffalo—I don't remember exactly. A stuffed penguin mounted on a stand was lying on its side and there was a case full of huge bird eggs, like ostrich or emu eggs. The trophies had seen better days. The deer heads were moth-eaten, with tufts of fur hanging from them, and a plastic eyeball presumably from one of the trophies lay in a corner of the room.

The servant led me to Booth's library, where Richard greeted me warmly, saying that Tom Loome had told him about the great things we were doing in Stillwater. Richard sat at a very old desk, and above him, on the wall, were a family crest and a pair of crossed swords. He was tallish, maybe six foot two, and somewhat stocky. "Portly" might be a better description. He wore glasses, and whenever I saw him these were either taped or so bent that they sat on his face at an angle. He always had an amused look on his face, like he was keeping a secret. He seemed genuinely interested in the people he met—very curious about what they did.

We talked about his book town "movement" and the small towns around the world selling used books to revive their economies. He showed me his own book collections. One was hundreds of books with the word "Hay" in the title—that was all a book needed to be included—so there were books on hay baling, the properties of hay, what animals eat hay, what to do with hay in the winter, and how to grow hay along the side of the road. He also had a big collection of books on Native

Americans, including some very rare original volumes about Henry Schoolcraft's expedition to discover the source of the Mississippi River.

When it was time for dinner, we went into a large dining room with a long table. Three more servants, all wearing garage jumpsuits, stood to the side, silent, while I and a couple of other guests ate cold soup and a mysterious meat pie. Richard seemed to enjoy the company and talked nonstop about rural economies, book towns, and the Welsh government, which he despised. He recounted the story of how he declared Hay an independent kingdom and about his horse, the prime minister. Richard had an antiestablishment bent and was critical of local governments for their failure to preserve the rural way of life. "All small rural towns were based on a food economy," he said in an interview in 1998, "but they got rid of that and gave us a tourist economy. Eighty percent of it went to big business: to theme parks, package tours, to chain motels, what have you." He was entertaining and genuine, if a bit odd.

You have to hand it to Richard. He bought books libraries in the United Kingdom and the United States were throwing out, gathered them together in a small town, and then promoted the town so people came and bought the books. A simple and effective plan. Even though Hay today only has a population of 1,500, over three hundred thousand people visit the town every year—the Hay book festival alone draws two hundred thousand—and twenty bookstores are still in operation. Richard Booth was made an MBE (Member of the Most Excellent Order of the British Empire) by Queen Elizabeth in 2004 for his work reviving small towns and is a legend in the secondhand book business. He recounted his life in an autobiography called *My Kingdom of Books*. He died on August 20, 2019, at the age of eighty.

12. The Mormon
and the Map Thief

Judge not
lest ye be judged yourself.
METALLICA

As MY TRIPS to Archer City and Hay-on-Wye show, there was a Wild West quality to the used book business in the 1980s and 1990s. A book dealer with a decent idea could take over an entire town. Based on the number of book-related crimes that occurred during this time, a surprising number of criminals seemed to adopt this same no-holds-barred attitude.

Drawn by the rising prices of rare books and maps that began in the late 1970s, these crooks stole books, forged documents, and tore maps from their ancient bindings with abandon, not restrained, as they might be today, by national databases or instant information. In chapter 4, I described a few criminals I had some direct contact with, like Stephen Blumberg and John Jenkins, but I had a glancing familiarity with others. Two that come to mind are Mark Hofmann, a Mormon rare book dealer who murdered two people to cover up his extensive forgeries, and E. Forbes Smiley III, a respected map dealer who cut maps worth millions of dollars out of rare library books.

The Mark Hofmann story came from a call I got from a woman who claimed she had a first edition of the Book of Mormon, one of the "black tulips" of the rare book business. This was published in 1830, recent enough to still be around, in a binding that could easily be mistaken for a just another old book, except in the early 1990s a first edition was worth over $60,000. Every so often you'd hear of one turning up at a flea market or in the attic of a distant relative of Joseph Smith, the founder of Mormonism.

This woman said she was related to Brigham Young,[1] who led the Mormons to Salt Lake City after Joseph Smith was murdered in Illinois in 1844. She said an uncle of hers had treasured the book his entire life. "Oh, sure," I thought, "probably just a reprint." But I certainly wanted to see it and asked her to bring it in.

Before she did, she, alas, discovered the book might be worth thousands and decided to send it to an auction, but she did let me see it. It really was a first edition. I offered to either handle the sale for her or pay $15,000 in cash, but it was too late: she had already made arrangements with some other scalawag.

While researching the Book of Mormon, I ran across Hofmann, who, in the early 1980s, engineered a series of forgeries that duped some of the most prominent booksellers, autograph dealers, and forensic scientists in the country. When his crimes were about to be exposed, he tried to create a distraction by killing two prominent businesspeople with pipe bombs.

He was able to pull off the first part—the duping part—because the Mormons, or, more precisely, the members of the Church of Jesus Christ of Latter-day Saints (LDS), are interested in anything related to the founding of their church. To make a long story short, the LDS Church was founded when an angel named Moroni appeared to Joseph Smith in 1826 in western New York and told him where to dig up some golden plates that had Egyptian hieroglyphics etched on them. Smith

---

[1] As are many others. Young had fifty-five wives and sired nearly sixty children.

was ordered by Moroni to translate these into what would become the Book of Mormon. Since this event was relatively recent, many diaries, testimonials, visions, revelations, and denunciations about it still existed in the 1970s. Unfortunately for the LDS Church, some of these documents contained accounts of bad behavior by Joseph Smith, a known charlatan, drinker, gambler, and womanizer. The church was eager to publicize materials that supported the miracle of its founding but preferred to suppress, if possible, any unfounded or ugly rumors.

Mark Hofmann enters the picture in the late 1970s as a geeky-looking guy with long hair and big glasses who studied Mormon history at the University of Utah in Salt Lake City. He was from a devout Mormon family but while on a mission trip to England became disillusioned with, even hostile toward, the Mormon Church. As he studied Mormon documents in the college library, he paid particular attention to records the church might be missing. He realized that if some of these magically appeared—say, by being forged—they might confirm or contradict details about the founding of Mormonism.

The young Hofmann, who was kind of an evil genius, saw this as a field ripe for exploitation: handwriting samples of early Mormon converts were limited, not many Mormon forgeries were around, and original documents were selling for high prices. The more controversial the documents were, the better. Hofmann's plan was to introduce his forgeries in a calculated way, first to gain the church's confidence and then, in essence, to blackmail it.

His first forgery, in 1979, was a five-by-seven sheet of paper that described a secret anointing blessing used by the Mormon Church that had never, prior to this, appeared in print. When Hofmann showed it to Jeff Simmonds, the special collections librarian at the University of Utah, Simmonds was quite excited about the find and bought the blessing from Hofmann for sixty dollars. "A short time later, Hofmann brought in another handwritten document," wrote Linda Sillitoe and Allen D. Roberts in their 1988 book *Salamander: The Story of the Mormon Forgery Murders*. "This was a letter from Joseph Smith to two young sisters, Maria and Sarah Lawrence. The text was intimate, heavily implicating the Prophet in polygamy with the teenage sisters, for whom he was legal guardian at the time." Simmonds thought this letter looked like fake anti-Mormon propaganda and wouldn't buy it, but the two incidents mark the beginning of Hofmann's career as a forger.

Hofmann's first significant Mormon forgery was of a document called the Anthon Transcript—so named because Smith's scribe, Martin Harris, showed something like it to Columbia professor Charles Anthon in 1828—that Hofmann claimed he found pasted into a seventeenth-century King James Bible. It was a folded piece of paper with Egyptian characters supposedly copied by Smith directly from the golden plates. Several experts authenticated this forgery, and the church, believing the paper confirmed the story of its founding, traded Hofmann $20,000 worth of rare Mormon items for it.

Based on this "discovery," Hofmann, twenty-six at the time, quit school and started his own rare book business that specialized in Mormon history. His next notable forgery was a paper claiming Joseph Smith had designated his son Joseph III as his successor and not, as the church maintained, Brigham Young. If true, this would disrupt the entire hierarchy of the Mormon Church, and Hofmann figured the people in charge would pay plenty to suppress it. When the church balked at his original price, he offered the paper to an anti-Mormon faction, at which point the LDS relented and accepted his terms.

Over the next few years Hofmann generated a steady stream

of other, minor, forgeries, but in 1984 he produced another earthshaking document that came to be known as the Salamander Letter. This letter said that when Joseph Smith dug up the golden plates, they were not guarded by the angel Moroni, as Smith had claimed, but by a white salamander (the symbolism of which is too involved for our humble purposes here). The church at first questioned the letter's authenticity but, after subjecting it to extensive tests, eventually bought it through a local businessman and devout Mormon named Steve Christensen.[2] "If I can produce something so correctly, so perfect that the experts declare it genuine," Hofmann once said in describing his forgeries, "then for all practical purposes it is genuine."

Hofmann also sold non-Mormon forgeries, including letters and signatures of George Washington, Abraham Lincoln, Mark Twain, and John Milton. He spent more money than he made: buying first editions, purchasing a house in an exclusive part of Salt Lake City, and bidding on rare book collections. By 1985 he was over $1 million in debt.

To get out of the hole, Hofmann created his most spectacular forgery yet, a single sheet of paper called the "Oath of a Freeman," which he claimed he found while browsing in a bookstore in New York City. This was a legendary document, described but never seen, thought to be the first piece of paper printed in America in 1638. When Hofmann offered it to the Library of Congress for $1.5 million, the library said the discovery "would be one of the most important and exciting finds of the century" and "found nothing inconsistent with a mid-seventeenth century attribution."

---

[2] The church was, apparently, an easy mark. In 2005 it was reported that the LDS Church owned 446 Hofmann forgeries that it either bought from Hofmann or acquired elsewhere.

Delays in selling the "Oath of a Freeman" caused Hofmann to get behind on his debt payments. To raise funds, he contacted the LDS Church and claimed he was about to buy the papers of William E. McLellin, an early LDS convert who became a rabid anti-Mormon after he broke with Joseph Smith in 1838. These papers supposedly showed that Smith tried to sell the copyright to the Book of Mormon for whiskey money; that Emma Smith, his first of several wives, didn't believe his story about seeing the angel Moroni; and that McLellin had walked in on Joseph Smith while he was having relations with a servant girl.

The church did not want the scandalous McLellin papers to see the light of day, so it again asked Steve Christensen to act as a go-between to secure the papers. Christensen cosigned a $185,000 loan for Hofmann to buy this nonexistent collection, and Hofmann used the money to pay off other debts. When the deadline for producing the McLellin papers drew near, and the bank loan came due, Hofmann decided he needed a distraction, so he built three pipe bombs. He delivered one to Christensen and one to Gary Sheets, another prominent businessman. The third bomb was in Hofmann's car when it went off by mistake, causing Hofmann to inadvertently blow himself up. Christensen and Sheets's wife, Kathy—who picked up the package addressed to her husband that contained the pipe bomb—were killed. Hofmann survived, but once his forgeries were revealed, he probably wished he hadn't.

This is the barest outline of Hofmann's story, chronicled, if you're interested, in at least seven books, numerous articles, and a true crime documentary on Netflix. In the early 2000s the Southwestern Association of Forensic Document Examiners called Hofmann the best forger of the last 1,200 years: he was able to imitate eighty-six historic signatures, make his own ink, age his own paper, and engrave his own postmarks.

"He had his documents authenticated by the best: The Library of Congress, the American Antiquarian Society, the FBI, the University of California, and the McCrone Research Institute," said George Throckmorton, one of the examiners who studied Hofmann's methods. At his 1987 trial, Hofmann pled guilty to two counts of murder and two counts of forgery and was sentenced to life in prison.

My twice-removed connection to the map thief, E. Forbes Smiley III, came after his arrest in 2005 made national news. A customer of mine called and said he had purchased a map from Smiley's gallery in New York City in the late 1980s and wondered if the map he had might be one of the maps that had been stolen. When he described it to me—a common map of Minnesota from the 1880s that he paid less than a hundred dollars for—I told him I doubted this was one of the multithousand-dollar maps that Smiley ripped from rare books at libraries across the country.

As you might guess from his name, E. Forbes Smiley III was not your average dude. As one of his customers noted, "If you're looking for a guy who the average American thinks is a preppy who went to Andover and then to Yale and is just about to go play golf, that's Forbes." At the time of his arrest, Smiley was one of the most respected map dealers in the country. He revered maps, had an encyclopedic knowledge of mapmakers, and was for a time the leading expert on early North American maps in the world.

When Smiley got into the map business in the mid-1970s, the market was limited and the prices modest. The field took off when high-end decorators started buying original maps for their wealthy clients. "The growth in the market led to a plague of 'atlas-breaking' as the maps in the books became more valuable than the books themselves," wrote William Finnegan in the *New Yorker*.

This map rush did not escape the notice of criminals, who found fertile hunting grounds in the unguarded rare book rooms of university and public libraries. If you knew what you were looking for and could fill out a call slip, you had access to books that contained maps worth thousands of dollars. The map in, for example, John Smith's 1631 *Advertisements for the Unexperienced Planters of New England* might be an after-thought for librarians but could, by itself, sell for over $50,000. According to Miles Harvey's *The Island of Lost Maps*, "Well into the 1990s many university libraries lacked surveillance cameras for even their most rare and valuable collections."

Into this upwardly mobile market stepped Smiley, who knew more about maps than just about anyone in the country. In 1984 he opened his own gallery in New York City called North American Maps & Autographs. Even though he was barely scraping by, Smiley projected an aristocratic image and hinted he came from old-world money. According to one of his associates, "He certainly didn't have any shortage of self-esteem. He'd call and make it known that he was calling 'from the Vineyard.'" (He had a place on Martha's Vineyard, de-scribed as "a dump—a tiny, dark, egg-shaped cabin in Chil-mark, at the western end of the island.")

Smiley's gallery attracted well-heeled customers who he convinced to develop noteworthy collections. His first big fish was Norman Leventhal, a wealthy real estate developer who put together an extensive collection of maps related to Massa-chusetts that he later donated to the Boston Public Library. An-other customer was Lawrence Slaughter, who collected English maps, charts, globes, atlases, and other books related to colo-nial North America. That collection now resides in the New York Public Library.

As he rose in the business Smiley earned a reputation for his uncanny ability to turn up rare and unusual maps, but the higher he rose, the more secretive, arrogant, and, some said, unethical he became. William Reese, a New Haven, Connecticut, map dealer, said Smiley once bought a rare atlas from him with a bad check, got on a train back to New York, and during the trip ripped the atlas apart so he could sell the individual maps as soon as he got back to his gallery. Another major map dealer, Graham Arader from Philadelphia, clashed with Smiley numerous times and was always suspicious of him. The *New Yorker*'s William Finnegan reported in 2005 that "Arader readily recites a list of major collectors whom he believes Smiley 'stole' from him" and "says that the only reason Smiley could 'undercut' him was that he was a thief."

Smiley's goal was to become, in fact and not just in appearance, a member of the upper class. He tore down his shack on Martha's Vineyard and was in the process of replacing it with a modular, modernistic house—an eyesore, according to the locals—when construction was halted due to unpaid taxes. The *New Yorker* article relates that in 2005, "The place is still a shambles. The contractor abandoned the project and the kitchen, imported from Italy, is still crated in the basement. He and his family are living there without running water."

Smiley also financed a utopian dream in Sebec, Maine, where he owned an old farmhouse. Like the booksellers who took over entire towns, Smiley wanted to create his own ideal community. He bought and renovated several old buildings in Sebec, including the post office and a general store that featured an old-style candy counter and soda fountain and sold gourmet coffee and earthenware mixing bowls. "Largely encouraged by many local residents of Sebec," Smiley wrote in the *Piscataquis Observer,* "I have taken on this project in the hope that its success will add in a small way to the health and prosperity of the town as a whole." According to Michael Blanding in his book *The Map Thief,* "By local estimates, Smiley spent $600,000 on the renovations alone, and thousands more every week on payroll during the summer."

To cover these expenses, Smiley had to move a lot of high-priced merchandise, and he later said it was his mounting debts that forced him into a life of crime. He claims he stole his first map from the Sterling Memorial Library at Yale in 2002: "The Sterling Library is the first place I realized I had access to material that was not well catalogued," he told Blanding. "I am looking at a piece of paper that I can fold and put in my pocket, that people in New York expect me to show up with because I've been doing this for twenty-five years legitimately. And I can get thirty thousand dollars wired up to Maine this afternoon."

Others suspect he was stealing maps well before 2002, but the Sterling Library theft was the first time anyone connected the dots. In July of 2002 Margit Kaye, a librarian at the Sterling, noticed a map on Smiley's website that had a smudge in the corner that she recognized.[3] "Oh my God," she thought. "That's our map." She checked the records for other books and map folders that Smiley had examined, and, sure enough, more maps were missing; some were even for sale on Smiley's website. When she brought this to the attention of the library's director, though, he said there was nothing they could do about it without direct proof.

That direct proof came on June 8, 2005, while Smiley was in the Beinecke Rare Book and Manuscript Library, also at Yale University, where he had requested several rare atlases he said he wanted to study in preparation for the very prestigious London Map Fair. According to people who knew him, he was, by

---

[3] Note the convergence of the early days of the internet and this incident. Smiley had created his website a month before Kaye recognized the map.

now, harried, sweaty, paranoid, and in poor health. On that June day, he couldn't stop coughing. When he pulled out his handkerchief, Blanding writes in *The Map Thief,* "an X-Acto knife blade wrapped inside fell softly to the carpeted floor. He folded the cloth and put it back into his pocket, oblivious to what had just happened."

When Smiley left the room to take a break, Naomi Saito, a librarian at the Beinecke, conducted a routine check and noticed the blade lying on the floor. She picked it up in a tissue and brought it to her supervisor, Ellen Cordes, who became quite alarmed: finding an X-Acto blade in a rare book room was like finding a blowtorch in a bank. As Cordes looked through the book request cards she focused on E. Forbes Smiley III, a name she recognized. She looked him up on the internet, saw he was a map dealer, and contacted the Sterling Library to see if they knew anything about him. Bad news. The Sterling said they had long suspected Smiley of stealing maps but hadn't been able to prove it. In the meantime, Cordes noticed, Smiley had returned to the rare book room.

Cordes called the head of security, who kept an eye on Smiley while Cordes checked some books he had already returned. Maps were missing, including the map in John Smith's 1631 *Advertisements for the Unexperienced Planters of New England.* Convinced that Smiley had stolen them, Cordes contacted Detective Martin Buonfiglio from the Yale Police Department. By the time Detective Buonfiglio got to the library, Smiley had left, so Buonfiglio decided to go after him. Once he caught him, Buonfiglio confronted Smiley with the X-Acto blade and Cordes's concerns about the missing maps. He checked Smiley's briefcase and found several maps that Smiley claimed were his personal property. Buonfiglio told Smiley he'd have to come back to the library and sort the maps out.

When Ellen Cordes looked at the maps in Smiley's briefcase,

she immediately recognized the John Smith map because it had, written in pencil, the name of one Henry C. Taylor, a benefactor of the Beinecke Library. Buonfiglio also went over the library's security footage and saw Smiley tearing the world map out of the 1578 *Speculum Orbis Terrarum* atlas—a map worth, at the time, $200,000. All told, four maps in the briefcase belonged to the Beinecke, but several others didn't.

The implications of this were clear to Cordes. Here was a respected map dealer, granted access to every rare book room on the East Coast, with upwards of $500,000 of stolen maps in his possession. At that point Detective Buonfiglio arrested Smiley, charged him with grand larceny, and reported the case to the FBI's art crimes division.

Smiley's arrest sent shock waves through the map community. To this day, no one knows how many maps he stole. "My guess is that five percent have been returned," Graham Arader told the *New York Times*. "I'd been telling everybody that Forbes was a crook for twenty years." Dealers speculated that some of the maps in the collections Smiley developed early in his career for Norman Leventhal and Laurence Slaughter in the 1980s may also have been stolen. Many libraries, because they did not catalog the maps separately, did not even know they'd been victimized. For his part, Smiley admitted to stealing ninety-four of the nearly three hundred maps that various libraries claimed were missing. In 2005, he was sentenced to three and a half years in federal prison and ordered to pay $2 million in restitution.

13. North America's
First Book Town

Remember the forest that
grows from fallen trees.
SAMANTHA HUNT

GIVEN THE ANEMIC STATE of the secondhand business
now, it's hard to believe that book towns like Archer City
and Hay-on-Wye even existed—they were a testament to the
popularity of the used book business in the 1990s. Stillwater
would also become a book town, but in order to do that, it
needed a lot more booksellers. In late 1992 there were only
three, and one of them, Jim Cummings, was about to leave.
Jim had decided to sell his interest in 232 South Main to Tom
Loome and me in early 1993 because, with three people all buying books, the St. Croix store had become too crowded. Shortly
after he left, Tom and I started the Stillwater Book Center, and
the number of booksellers in town increased exponentially.

The idea for the Book Center came to me while Jim was
packing up his books and the large clothing store directly across
the street from us went out of business—a trend then in downtown Stillwater. Stores in business for years—clothing stores,
hardware stores, and drugstores—shut down as Walmart and
other chain stores moved into the area. Stillwater did better
than other small towns because of the tourists, who supported
new restaurants, retail stores, and antique shops. As I looked
over at the empty space, I thought it would make a great book
collective (basically a mall, only with booksellers) like one I

had seen out east. I suggested this to Tom, and he took to the idea immediately. We outlined what putting together such a mall would involve and figured there would be room for about thirty dealers. We'd need at least fifteen to get the idea off the ground.

By this time, St. Croix Books was the envy of the Twin Cities book world. Who ever thought tourists would buy used books? The more refined dealers still thought selling secondhand books to the ragged masses was undignified, but fifteen of the more opportunistic ones were willing to try a space at the Center. We signed them up and took out a three-year lease on the clothing store, which was about the same size (4,500 square feet) as 232 South Main. Signing up the next fifteen was harder, and I have to hand it to Tom: he contacted every bookseller in Minnesota, Iowa, Illinois, and Wisconsin and convinced enough of them that if they did not rent a space in the new Stillwater book mall, their bookselling careers were as good as over.

When the Book Center opened at the beginning of 1994, it had thirty booksellers and ninety thousand books, including specialists in military history (Paul Kisselburg), cookbooks, the East (Greg Gamradt), hunting and fishing (Ken Czech), children's, philosophy, and automobiles (Tom Warth).[1] The University of Minnesota, the Minnesota Historical Society, and the Hill Monastic Manuscript Library all put their new publications in the Book Center, and several general booksellers,

---

[1] We hired a general manager and regular staff to run the store: Charles Perry, Zantha Warth, and Art Hudgins. They were great people, our friends as well as our employees, and the Book Center would not have been the success it was without them. In an introductory speech to incoming booksellers I also thanked, among other people, Dwight Cummins, our friend and local lawyer who put together the complicated contracts we needed for the leases at the Center.

The Stillwater Book Center.

like Powell's Books from Chicago, had spaces. Since it was the only book mall in the Midwest and one of only two or three in the country, it generated a lot of publicity. When the Minneapolis *Star Tribune* did an article, the reporter contacted Jacob Chernofsky, the editor of the *AB Bookman's Weekly.* "To put together 30 booksellers in a town of that size [15,000 people] is extremely unusual in this country," Chernofsky said by phone. "That would be phenomenal."

It was probably due to Tom's background as a college professor that we had lectures about books and bookselling at the Book Center. We usually had forty or fifty people attend these talks, which is a pretty good turnout as those things go. The Book Center booksellers loved them because they brought in hard-core book lovers and collectors, who always bought books. We managed to roust Melvin McCosh from his squalor on Lake Minnetonka to talk about the history of secondhand bookselling in Minnesota. Despite being in frail health, Melvin did a very good job; his talk followed the story line covered in the earlier section about him in chapter 6. Pat Coleman, the acquisitions librarian for the Minnesota Historical Society, came and talked about some of the remarkable books he had found for the society.

Pat later recalled that McCosh had written a few hundred pages about the history of bookselling in Minnesota, but those disappeared after he died. (Steve Anderson thinks McCosh's daughter might have them.) This was a big loss, because the only other account ever written about bookselling in Minnesota was a short life of the rare book dealer Edmund Brooks, called *Of Brooks and Books,* written by Lee Edmonds Grove and published by the University of Minnesota Press in 1945.

Jack Parker, the first curator of the James Ford Bell Library from 1953 until 1991, gave a talk about Bell, a singular figure in the history of Minnesota book collecting. Bell made a fortune in the flour business and lived on Lake Minnetonka in the 1920s and 1930s in, no doubt, a nicer mansion than Melvin McCosh's. He donated his collection of books about the fur trade and Upper Midwest businesses to the University of Minnesota in 1953; two significant items in the collection are the first printed edition of *The Travels of Marco Polo,* printed in Germany in 1477, and the famous 1507 Martin Waldseemüller twelve-panel globe, pictured in slices (called gores, representing the curvature of the earth) and the first map to use the name America.

Eric Hollas, the director of the Hill Monastic Manuscript Library (HMML) at St. John's University, came and explained that the library's mission was to photograph and preserve endangered handwritten manuscripts. The HMML was founded in 1965 in response to the loss of books and manuscripts from

European libraries during the two World Wars. They first pho-tographed Christian manuscripts but later included Islamic and Jewish manuscripts from places like Harar, Ethiopia, and the Old City of Jerusalem. The library contains over 140,000 digi-tized copies, comprising forty million handwritten pages.

Donald Jackson, senior illuminator to the Crown Office of Queen Elizabeth, came to sign copies of his book, *The Story of Writing,* and to talk about the history of calligraphy. During his talk, he mentioned his desire to someday create a handwritten illuminated Bible. Later, in 1995, Jackson discussed this project with the aforementioned Eric Hollas. One thing led to another, and St. John's officially commissioned the *St. John's Bible* in 1999, which was to be the first handwritten and illuminated Bible since the invention of the printing press. The project took twelve years and included a team of theologians, calligraphers, illuminators, and artists. It was completed in 2011.

St. John's produced a Heritage Edition of the Bible, limited to 299 copies and priced at $145,000. The original is thought to be worth millions. You could say that this was a project that Tom and I helped put together, but we have yet to see a dime of the profits.

After my trips to Hay-on-Wye and Archer City, it occurred to me that with thirty dealers and 90,000 books in the Stillwa-ter Book Center, St. Croix Antiquarian with 120,000 books, Loome Theological with 250,000 books, and Jim Cummings with 100,000 books in his house, Stillwater had 500,000 books within a four-block area. Paul also had a small store, Kisselburg Military Books, with 10,000 books. And Stillwater, even though it was twenty minutes from the Twin Cities, was technically a small town with 15,000 people. That's a book town, according to Richard Booth's definition.

I suggested to Tom in February 1994 that we ask Richard to make Stillwater an official Book Town, an idea Tom was surprised he hadn't thought of himself, since he had spent so much time in Hay. When he called Booth and outlined our proposal, Richard was as enthusiastic about it as we were. There were other book towns, like in France and Scotland, but none so far in the United States.[2] A North American book town would mean a lot of publicity for Richard's movement.

In August 1994 Richard Booth came to Stillwater and declared it "North America's First Book Town." We went all out for the dedication ceremony: signs, a brass quartet, free wine and hors d'oeuvres. The mayor and other city notables attended. Booth wore his ceremonial fake ermine–trimmed red cloak and the rabbit fur crown he had decorated with a magic marker and carried his gold spray-painted toilet bowl orb. I have a picture of Richard and the mayor at the time, Charles Hooley, sitting together at St. Croix Books. Richard is leaning back, belly protruding. Charles Hooley is wearing a suit and tie and his shoes gleam from the light in the store. Both men, in their fifties, look into the camera and beam like they've discovered a cure for cancer.

During the ceremony, Richard presented us with a framed document, done in calligraphy and certified with his personal seal: *"I, Richard Booth, King of Hay, Lord of all Booktowns and their Protector in perpetuity, Hereby Declare that Stillwater, Minnesota is the first Booktown in the Western Hemisphere. Let no one gainsay or dare to dispute this is my official decree."* The publicity from the declaration was tremendous. There were feature articles in the Minneapolis and St. Paul

---

[2] Archer City had not fulfilled Booth's book town requirements and thus was not an "official" book town.

Stillwater mayor Charles Hooley and King Richard Booth.

papers and shorter mentions in the *New York Times* and *Washington Post*. Even now, over twenty years later, when you say you're from Stillwater in book circles, people will ask, "Say, isn't that the book town?"

Mary Ann Grossmann, the book editor for the *St. Paul Pioneer Press,* covered the event this way:

Richard Booth, self-proclaimed King of Hay, is described by his Stillwater friends Tom Loome and Gary Goodman as "scruffy-looking, decadent, a character, a perfect British eccentric." Booth, who is in his 50s, lives and works in Hay-on-Wye, a tiny town of just over 1,000 people on the Welsh-English border. Like Stillwater, Hay is a beautiful river town. Booth operates out of his castle, a twelfth-century Norman structure with big looming

walls that is filled with books, but he owns bookstores
in other towns as well. King Richard, who "rules" since
he declared Hay independent from Great Britain, first
thought of the Book Town idea more than 20 years ago
when formerly prosperous shops in little market towns
such as Hay-on-Wye declined as supermarkets became
popular across Europe. Why not, he asked, fill those
empty shops with used bookstores? Hay-on-Wye became the first Book Town in 1961, followed by one in
Belgium, two in France, one in Holland and another in
Switzerland. The basic ingredients for a Book Town's
success . . . include a site of natural beauty, close proximity to a densely populated area, plenty of inexpensive
rental properties, and the support of local authorities.

Stillwater fulfills all those criteria. Booth's longtime
friend Loome says the King of Hay knows what he's doing.

King Richard in full regalia.

"Booth is not as mad as he likes to pretend he is," Loome says. "He's a pretty shrewd customer. He's got a lot of spit and vinegar. But he's not so weird he doesn't know there are advantages in cultivating that reputation."

Richard was thrilled with the attention. The day after the ceremony he held an audience at St. Croix Books, where he sat on a makeshift throne dressed in his royal regalia while booksellers and local businesspeople filed by and paid their respects. He was grandiose and particularly excited about the possibility of another North American Book Town in Trois-Pistoles, Canada, a small town on the St. Lawrence River north of Quebec City. One book scout was so overcome by the grandeur of it all—or so hungover from the free wine the night before—that he almost fainted and had to be revived by the orange juice and rolls we provided for the event.

Later, I took Richard to the warehouse where I had stored the books from San Antonio, in the hopes that I could, as Tom said, "unload" them on him. Booth regularly acquired vast quantities of books in the United States and shipped them back to Wales for his stores in Hay-on-Wye but didn't always pay for them. As Paul Kisselburg recalls, "Booth owed McCosh many thousands of dollars. Melvin owned an old schoolhouse in Dundas, Minnesota, near Northfield, that he filled with thousands of books. In the 1980s, he sold the books to Booth. Booth never paid. McCosh had some kind of legal judgment on Booth who had declared bankruptcy at least once thereafter. It is doubtful Melvin could have collected anything, but he was thinking about confronting Booth when the latter came to Stillwater."

As for the San Antonio books, Richard didn't want them. So now I had eleven thousand books in a rented warehouse

Big news in Stillwater. Courtesy of the Stillwater Gazette.

that, to add insult to injury, started leaking, so the books got soaked and swelled up and broke the metal bookcases they were stored on. It was an ungodly mess. I had to rent several dumpsters and throw them away, again proving my thesis that there's no such thing as a free book.

It was a lot of work managing the stores in downtown Stillwater. I was the main caretaker of St. Croix Antiquarian and the Stillwater Book Center and still traveled about a week a month. Tom wasn't as involved in the downtown stores because he had his own big operation up at the church. Keeping the thirty booksellers in the Book Center in line was like herding a bunch of socialist cats, so when two Book Center booksellers, Paul Kisselburg and Mark Douglas, offered to buy the business in 1995, we sold it to them.

This garnered front-page, Martian invasion–like headlines in the *Stillwater Gazette*: "Loome, Goodman Sell Book Center." The article reads, "Tom Loome and Gary Goodman, who have teamed to put Stillwater on the map as one of the premier book towns in the United States, have divested themselves of one of their jewels. 'We've been stretched too thin, to be honest,' said Loome, who, with Goodman, opened the Stillwater Book Center on Main Street last spring and have already built it into the best-known book center in the country."

We held the first annual Stillwater Book Fair two months later, on October 20, 1995—the day, by the way, that my sixth child, Steven, was born. Seven years before, Paul and I had hauled that monstrous bookcase to our first book fair in Chicago, and now Tom and I were hosting a fair of our own. Not everyone was happy about this. The Midwest Antiquarian Booksellers Association tried to claim that only associations—not individuals—could put on book fairs, but this turned out to be in the "unwritten rules" section of the booksellers' handbook and not a real thing.

Other booksellers may have been put off by our tawdry promotion of the secondhand book businesses in Stillwater, but thirty book dealers still signed up for that first Stillwater Book Fair. Several of the leading children's book specialists in the country were there, including Barbara Meyer Books of Texas, Maggie Page Books of Arkansas, and Arch Books of Minneapolis. Other exhibitors included Black Oak Books from California, specialists in scholarly books; Matthew Needle from Massachusetts, specialist in nineteenth-century books; and Fair Chase Books, specialists in big-game and sporting books. The night before the fair, we held a book auction that featured more than four hundred lots of books, including children's, sporting, western Americana, and natural history.

There couldn't have been a better setup for the booksellers and the local Stillwater businesses than a book fair. The sellers who came to town spent three days buying books, renting hotel rooms, and going out to eat. With a book festival that we also sponsored, the book fair, and the Book Town publicity, business increased dramatically: St. Croix Books did over $500,000 in business in 1995.

Even after we opened the Book Center and Stillwater became an official Book Town, my life on the road continued. I traveled while Mary Pat wrangled the six kids. Sometimes I drove through Nebraska, Iowa, Missouri, Illinois, and Wisconsin, or I would fly to New Jersey, rent a car, and drive to Connecticut, New York, Massachusetts, New Hampshire, Maine, Delaware, Pennsylvania, Ohio, and Washington, DC. I went to Seattle, Portland, San Francisco, and Los Angeles. I went to Vancouver, Calgary, Edmonton, Winnipeg, Toronto, Montreal, Ottawa, and Halifax. (The Appendix at the end of this book reproduces portions of a journal I kept while on some of these trips.) Over the years I covered the entire United States and Canada more than once. And I bought a lot of books. By now I had fifteen thousand—a far cry from the thousand I had started with.

14. The Book Collectors

Obsessive book collecting is the only
hobby that has a disease named after it.
NICHOLAS BASBANES

A s MY OWN TRIPS SHOW, one characteristic of these old booksellers is how much they traveled. Another is the dedication some put into developing personal collections. They found things and put them together in ways no institution or future bookseller can hope to replicate. Quoting, again, A. S. W. Rosenbach, "It is wonderful and magnificent that the gathering of books in this country is . . . not in the hands of college professors and great scholars. It is paradoxical, but true, that not a single library in the world has been formed by a great scholar." As Bernard McTigue, the rare books librarian at the New York Public Library, is quoted as saying in Nicholas Basbanes's *A Gentle Madness,* "Private collectors have always been the people who put the pieces together. It is their passion that builds these collections."

A prime example of this is our friend Paul Kisselburg. The General traveled incessantly, and over thirty years he amassed what is arguably one of the finest collections of military books in the world. Paul regularly went to England to buy books and reluctantly, grudgingly, let me tag along. On these trips I was, at best, a mere object to the General, a nuisance barely tolerated.[1]

---

[1] Paul did not have such a cold heart when it came to dachsunds. He had eight wiener dogs. He'd call home and have his wife put the phone up to the dogs' ears so they could hear his voice. These were not children. They were wiener dogs.

Still, as I learned from my trip to Wales in 1993, it was hard to travel and buy books in England when you were alone, so I suffered his degradations in silence.

Stillwater had stronger ties to England than any other town in the United States because of its connection to the Book Town movement. Tom traveled there often, and in 1996 Paul and I started going to the military book fairs held twice a year in York and Tunbridge Wells, usually in March and September. Our trips ran from 1996 to 2002 and likely coincided with the last period in history that booksellers could go out and still buy books not contaminated by the internet.

Tunbridge Wells and York are classic English towns and worth describing. Tunbridge is about forty miles southeast of London, a spa town that became popular in the seventeenth century, when wealthy people went to "take the waters" at a chalybeate spring discovered in 1606. (Chalybeate water is mineral water that contains salts of iron and has a distinctive reddish tint.) A physician connected to Dudley North, the discoverer of the spring, supposedly claimed the waters contained vitriol and could cure "the colic, the melancholy, and the vapors; it made the lean fat, the fat lean; it killed flat worms in the belly, loosened the clammy humors of the body, and dried the over-moist brain."

Shops were built near the springs beside a paved public walk, or promenade, called the Pantiles, named for clay paving stones that were baked in a pan. Tradesmen along the promenade dealt in high-class items, particularly Tunbridge ware, a kind of decoratively inlaid woodwork. In the 1800s Tunbridge Wells became Royal Tunbridge Wells because it was a favorite destination of Queen Victoria and Prince Albert. The town, with many buildings dating from the eighteenth and nineteenth centuries, was still a popular tourist destination when Paul and I started going there in 1996.

York, our other destination, is a walled city on the River Ouse about four hours north of London founded by the Romans in 71 CE and inhabited, at various times, by the Vikings, the Anglo-Saxons, and the Normans. It was central to the defense of the southern part of England and was sacked and burned several times in the process of changing hands. The town is known for its famous historical landmarks, such as York Minster, a large Gothic cathedral that took 250 years to build, and the city walls begun by the Romans and added to in the Middle Ages. The Shambles, an old street in York mentioned in the Domesday Book of 1086, has timber-framed buildings that date back to the 1300s. Some York merchants claim this street was the model for the fictional Diagon Alley, the magical market street in the Harry Potter books by J. K. Rowling, although Rowling disputes this. In the 1990s the street was filled with fine English shops, but when I went back recently, half the stores were hawking either Harry Potter merchandise or magical concoctions—think of newts in jars or crystals that grow your hair—so the street has lost its old-time charm. The locals, it must be said, are none too happy about it.

Paul and I would start our book-buying trips by going to the book fair at either York or Tunbridge Wells and then after it was over travel to other parts of the country; we might head to Manchester on one trip or Portsmouth the next. Paul remembers one shop called the Tin Drum that we stopped at in Norfolk on our way to York: "We went there during our first trip. It was a fantastic shop for you. I boxed up about ten boxes. Remember, I was merely your facilitator. He did not have much for me. I remember it was in the evening. My notes say I bought two boxes; you, seven. Subsequently, he moved his shop from Fakenham to a town on the coast, and we went there a year or so later. You bought some things, but it was not as good. I see that I or we spent £3,909. The pound at that time was always around $1.65 or so." Paul arranged for a trucking company to pick up the books we bought at different stores across the country. He numbered each of his boxes and, curiously, opened them in precise order when they got back to Stillwater.

There were good books in England then at reasonable prices. Nearly every small and medium town had an established secondhand bookstore, and the British dealers didn't pick the stores over like dealers did in the United States. These out-of-the-way stores didn't take credit cards, so you had to either have a British checking account or pay for the books in cash. The big shot, Paul, carried around wads of British pounds that, when he flashed them, made the British booksellers think they had died and gone to heaven.

It was amazing what you'd run into in England in those days. At one store, I bought the three-volume first-edition set of the Lord of the Rings trilogy by J. R. R. Tolkien. It was in fine condition, with flawless dust jackets, and priced at £495 (about $800 then). This was well before the movies came out. When the books made it back to the United States, I sold the set for $1,800—a bit less than the $40,000 the three volumes sell for now.

Paul bought World War II books for a fraction of what they would be in the United States. For a few years, he bought so many at the military book fairs that he was a sensation: when he walked in, the British dealers swarmed him like he was the Messiah and offered him all manner of rare books and manuscripts that they'd put aside especially for him. If he saw a book, like *The Latrine Habits of German Soldiers in World War II,* and didn't already own it, cost was no object. If it was a remainder—a book dumped on the market because it wasn't selling—and there were ten copies available, so much the better. He bought them all. He'd stand in the center of the room and dole out his British pounds to the masses crying for his attention.

Lest you think that all the dubious characters in the book business were from the United States, Paul remembers a guy he called—rather unkindly, I think—the Rat Man. As Paul describes him, "Rat Man was a smallish, dirty—or at least dressed in a dirty sweater and dirty wool half gloves—book dealer up in Yorkshire who looked like a rat. We went there on one of our trips to York. There was a large eighteenth- or nineteenth-century brick complex. I remember it had something to do with cotton. It was a massive structure with lots of small shops. There were at least two book dealers, one of which was a military dealer. You did spectacularly well at the Rat Man's shop. It was neat enough. No heat. Tall shelves. Very cheap."

Collectors like Paul and secondhand book dealers are one reason libraries even exist in their present form. Up until the invention of the printing press, the main repositories of classical knowledge were monasteries. These were, at best, poorly organized and, at worst, a neglected mess. Poggio Bracciolini, one of the great collectors of the Renaissance, felt justified in pillaging one monastery because the books "were not housed according to their worth, but were lying in most foul and obscure dungeon . . . a place into which condemned criminals would hardly have been thrust." Giovanni Boccaccio, the author of the *Decameron,* is thought to have ransacked another monastery library looking for unknown and uncataloged books. Many literary, philosophical, and historical works would have been lost if collectors and booksellers hadn't saved them.

The same is true of more ephemeral items: maps, atlases, journals, illustrations, newspapers, handbills. Many things regarded as disposable or utilitarian in their own time only survive today because they were saved by a far-sighted collector. Take chef and restaurateur Louis Szathmary, who owned the Bakery, a popular restaurant on Chicago's North Side. With the help of several Chicago booksellers he amassed thousands of items related to cooking that included menus, matchbooks, regional cookbooks, scarce pamphlets, and original manuscripts. Near the end of his life he donated this material to institutions around the country, including the University of Chicago and the University of Iowa. "Chef Louis" is revered in culinary circles for what he did to preserve so much of cooking history.

Or we could mention Hernando Colón, Christopher Columbus's second son. As Jason Daley wrote in a 2019 issue of *Smithsonian* magazine, Colón decided in the 1500s to collect "all books, in all languages and on all subjects, that can be found both within Christendom and without." By the time he was done he had collected between fifteen thousand and twenty thousand titles, a good portion of the total in existence at the time. According to Daley, "Unlike other collectors . . . Colón wasn't just interested in volumes from classical authors or other well-trodden texts—he bought everything he could find in print, including political pamphlets, guidebooks and posters from taverns."

So it was a privilege to witness the passion and dedication that Paul, like so many other booksellers of this era, put into his book collection. The same might be said about the theology books Tom Loome gathered together, Jim Cummings's diary collection, or Melvin McCosh's books on humor. Losing this process, in which individuals go out and develop collections and put them together in unique ways—not unlike how writers put together words—is a subtle, but significant, casualty of the internet.

15. The Stillwater Booktown Times

And such was the tenderness of his conscience, that a short
time before his death he expressed a regret for his having
been the author of fictions, which had passed for realities.
JAMES BOSWELL, *The Life of Samuel Johnson*

BEFORE MAKING THE TRANSITION to the dark days of
the internet, I have to mention the *Stillwater Booktown
Times*, a quarterly magazine Tom Loome and I started in 1996.
We used it as a news and propaganda tool to support the Book
Town and included in it, among other things, bookseller pro-
files and news about upcoming book-related events in Stillwater. It was only ten pages long, but even then we struggled to
find interesting or newsworthy items to write about, so sometimes we just made stuff up. One example is Colony 2000, an
idea that inadvertently prophesied some of the effects the internet would have on the used book business. Colony 2000 was
described as follows (in edited form):

Colony 2000, the retirement community for booksellers
being planned by St. Croix Antiquarian Books, received
its first major donation in July from the Northern Scandinavian Booksellers Association (NSBA). The $1,000.00
donated by the NSBA will go towards the purchase of an
eight-acre tract of land outside of Stillwater to create a
living and retreat facility for booksellers forced to retire
from active bookselling due to recent advances in technology. St. Croix Books has already secured the right of

first refusal for this property and is studying the possibilities for water and electricity. As its name suggests, Colony 2000 is scheduled to open in the year 2000 and will be able to accommodate thirty-five indigent booksellers.

This will be a living and working retreat for booksellers whose lives have been "broken on the rack of technology." It will be as self-sufficient as possible. When a bookseller is admitted, all books, personal property and other assets will be turned over to the Board of Governors, which will determine their proper placement. Colonists agree to remain for the duration of their working lives and to support the colony with a certain amount of compulsory labor. They should be in good health, be able to lift at least 50 pounds and have the stamina to work long hours in difficult conditions.

The main source of income for the colony will come from commercial ventures. Possible projects include handmade Book Town flags, coffee cups, dish towels, doormats, potholders, homemade wine, whiskey, jams, maple syrup and honey. The eight-acre site has some tillable land and forage for small animals such as chickens or pigs, but no open spaces for cattle or sheep. Residents will be given small plots of land to raise chickens and grow their own produce.

To generate the income necessary to pay rent, buy food, make payments on the communal debt, and provide the Board of Governors with a monthly stipend, colonists will need to work on these projects for at least forty hours a week. They will be paid in credits held in escrow at the colony store, which may be used to buy treats for the children or to purchase supplemental Book Town Medical Insurance that will cover major medical events such as broken arms, severed limbs, frostbite, bird flu, swine flu, and childbirth.

If there are any shortfalls, or if the Governors deem it necessary, colonists will need to work longer hours, including nights and weekends. Due to its proximity to the First Book Town in North America, Colony 2000 will likely become a tourist attraction, so colonists must be well groomed and present a cheerful demeanor at all times.

Despite being thinly disguised slavery, some people wondered if Colony 2000 was a real thing. One St. Paul bookseller was indignant that we claimed to have gotten a donation from the Northern Scandinavian Booksellers Association when no such organization existed. In response, Tom had a friend of his from the University of Minnesota write a letter of support for the colony in medieval Finnish. Another bookseller was ready to join, and a few others asked serious questions, like if there would be any vacation time. Like I've said before, it doesn't take a genius to be a bookseller.

The *Booktown Times* even got on Larry McMurtry's nerves at one point, or so I heard. McMurtry had taken to calling Archer City a Book Town but had not received Richard Booth's blessing to do so. In 1996, the *Booktown Times* took him to task:

> For the past eight years, Mr. McMurtry has quietly bought up property in his small (pop. 1500) hometown of Archer City, Texas and started no less than four bookstores. According to the *Fort Worth State-Telegram,* "Simply stated, McMurtry has decided to turn Archer City into an out-of-the way mecca for book collectors." In advertising we have seen, Archer City has unilaterally declared itself a Book Town.

There is no question that Archer City meets the criteria established by King Richard Booth, (i.e., it is a small town with a lot of books). However, none of the ceremonial and social obligations for making it an official book town have been met. There are such fine points as a formal petition to the King of Hay-on-Wye, the supplication and gifts delivered in person, the King's official visit and inspection of the proposed Book Town, the testimonials regarding character and, of great importance, the design of an official flag approved by the Scottish Genealogical Society. The other two Book Towns in North America, Stillwater and Trois-Pistoles (in Canada), have fulfilled these requirements faithfully. We shall assume that this third supposed Book Town, in Archer City, will follow the first two along this decent and honorable path. Meanwhile Thomas Loome and Gary Goodman, as Governors of the First Book Town in North America, await the customary and expected invitation to Archer City, along with the celebrations, expensive gifts, meals and entertainment that such invitations entail.

In the last issue of the *Booktown Times* we describe a Christmas party held at St. Croix Books, during which local businesses and book lovers came to celebrate the success of the Book Town. A member of the chamber of commerce gave a speech about how much the secondhand book business meant to Stillwater. The coming year, he said, would be even better. We did not know then that 1996 was not the beginning of a new age in secondhand bookselling but the beginning of the end.

16. The Beginning
of the End

The sorcerer is no longer able
to control the powers of the nether
world he has called up by his spells.
KARL MARX, *The Communist Manifesto*

FROM 1990 TO 1996, Tom Loome and I created a kind
of utopian bookselling community in Stillwater. The Book
Town designation, the Book Center, the book fairs, and the
Stillwater Booktown Times all brought attention to the town
and to the used book business. Tom sometimes referred to this
period as the "last golden age of bookselling in Minnesota."
But from 1997 to 2000, online selling platforms, especially
those developed by Amazon and eBay, began to exert a profound influence on the business, a business that had functioned
almost unchanged for six hundred years. This is when the machines—the cell phones, the personal computers, and the
internet—started to take over.

This process began earlier, in 1993, when a Seattle bookseller named Richard Weatherford developed Interloc, the first
online database for used and rare books. Interloc was, ironically, financed by booksellers themselves, who hoped it would
make the out-of-print book business more efficient. This turned
out to be a bad idea. Secondhand booksellers survived because
they had limited competition and a monopoly on finding out-
of-print books. With a database that listed the inventory of
bookstores across the country, they lost any power they had
over the market.

The consequences of this soon became evident. Before a centralized database, it could take years to find a copy of, say, *Killer Cats*. With a database, it could be located immediately. Even more destructive, from the booksellers' standpoint, was the race to the bottom caused by computer algorithms that automatically priced any new copy that came online a few cents lower than the next-cheapest copy. What was once a twenty-dollar book became a five-dollar book. Then a dollar book. Or a penny book.[1] The market for midrange books, a bookstore's bread and butter, collapsed. As more books were listed and the markets for particular books became saturated, sales dropped precipitously. Used booksellers were no longer just competing with the store down the block but with the whole world.

And then Amazon, that monster of retail, began selling secondhand books in 1997. Jeff Bezos, a Wall Street trader who felt he had missed out on the early-1990s internet boom, started Amazon in 1994 as an online bookstore in a rented house in Bellevue, Washington, with a quarter-million-dollar loan from his parents. After studying the market, he decided that books would be the best way for him to get into the internet game because of the large worldwide demand for literature, the low price points for books, and the number of titles available in print. Amazon sold its first book in 1995 and within two months was selling $20,000 a month to people in all fifty

---

[1] Today there are millions of books on Amazon, eBay, and AbeBooks for sale for a penny each. Massive book operations, like ThriftBooks and Sunrise Books, use algorithms to process used books and, when a book is priced at a penny, make money on the difference between what it costs them to ship the book and what, say, Amazon charges the customer for postage. "All told," says Mike Ward, the owner of ThriftBooks, "we only make a few cents on a penny book sale like that. But last year we sold almost twelve million books."

states. When Amazon started carrying used books, secondhand booksellers flocked to the site.

In 1995, the launch of the auction site eBay created another new way to sell books, and that continued the downward trend for the beleaguered bookseller. Pierre Omidyar, a French computer programmer, started eBay—called Auction Web at the time—in his living room, and the first item he sold was a broken laser pointer.[2] Concerned that his first customer might be disappointed, Omidyar called the bidder and asked if he knew the pointer was broken. To his dismay, the bidder said he collected broken laser pointers. Omidyar probably realized then that people, given the right circumstances, will buy almost anything: broken laser pointers, bottles of Elvis's sweat, pieces of toast that look like Jesus, or dog hair plucked from the original Lassie.

eBay took off in 1997, especially with toy collectors. Beanie Babies were hot that year and accounted for 10 percent of all of eBay's sales.[3] eBay started accepting used books in 1998, and, again, booksellers rushed to put books on the site. A lot of secondhand bookstores closed between 1998 and 2000, not because of financial difficulties but because it was easier to sell books on the internet. Why run a shop when you could sell books while you slept? It was a bookseller's bonanza, but

[2] A common myth about the beginning of eBay is that Omidyar started it to help his fiancée trade Pez dispensers, but this was a story invented by a public relations firm in order to get publicity for the company.

[3] When I went to the Major League Baseball All-Star Game in Denver in 1998 with Mark Ziegler, fans at the game received a red, white, and blue Beanie Baby called Glory the Bear. A woman at the entrance offered us $100 for our bears, which we gladly took. Other people (we noticed bitterly) were getting $200 and $300 for their bears. People also paid $50 for used ticket stubs, which they wanted to include with the Glory package. Today you can buy a Glory Bear on eBay, with a ticket stub, for $5.

it didn't last long. More books online made formerly scarce books common fodder, so prices, then sales, dropped dramatically. The saturation and instant gratification also dampened the enthusiasm of collectors, who enjoyed hunting for hard-to-find items; the thrill of the chase just wasn't there anymore. The same thing happened with antiques and toys, and those dealers, too, moaned about the effect eBay and Amazon had on their businesses.

By 1998 I was selling a thousand books a month through these platforms—which also included sites like Alibris (which absorbed Interloc) and the Advanced Book Exchange (ABE, now AbeBooks)—and had two full-time employees just processing the orders.[4] But I was clueless about what the impact of the internet would be on the book business, as illustrated by an article by James Romenesko in the *St. Paul Pioneer Press* in 1998: "Stillwater bookseller Gary Goodman says that predictions that the on-line world is going to kill small book retailers is flat out wrong. Just the opposite: Goodman's used and out-of-print book operation is so robust because of the Internet that he's hired two full time employees to only do Web work.

---

[4] My son Jonathan bought Little Golden Books (those small, illustrated children's books that are thirty or forty pages long) online or in local antique stores for almost nothing and sold them on eBay for hundreds of dollars. A Little Golden Book with a dust jacket, for example, sold for at least a hundred dollars. If it had an intact puzzle or some other gimmick, like the bandages for the Nurse Nancy book, it sold for a lot more. I never knew exactly what Jonathan did with all the money he made, but for a twelve-year-old boy he sure had a lot of tennis shoes. My son Nolan rooted around the store looking for things to put on eBay. Once he found a five-page playbill from 1860, priced at twenty dollars in the store, and noticed that one of the actors in the play was John Wilkes Booth, the actor who assassinated Abraham Lincoln. It sold for hundreds of dollars. Today Nolan buys and sells fine bindings on the internet under the name Under the Hill Books. When I showed him an early draft of this book, he said, "Then I must be the second-to-last bookseller."

'Internet orders have become half my business,' says Goodman, co-owner of St. Croix Antiquarian Booksellers and Midtown Books in downtown Stillwater. He notes that 99 percent of all titles are out-of-print and the large retailers usually don't stock them. They call people like Goodman to help fill these orders."

Online sales—as opposed to bookstore sales—stayed steady until about 2000 but started to drop after that. So many books came online that prices became standardized—a copy of *Killer Cats* was priced the same in Alaska as it was in Arkansas—and this made it harder for dealers to travel to other stores and find books they could resell at a profit. They couldn't just stock their stores with the books people brought in off the street either: the dog book section might be picked over, but people brought in cat books. And who wants cat books? Nobody. So the dog book people stopped coming.

At the same time, the value of the books booksellers already owned dropped like day-old doughnuts. Buyers used their phones to compare the prices of books in the stores with those on the internet, so you might have a book priced at forty dollars and a customer would say—usually loudly—that he could get it on Amazon for two. (I considered banning these devil's devices but was talked out of it by my kids, who said it would make me look like the old guy who yells at people to get off his lawn.[5]) When people brought in books to sell, they had looked them up and wanted $500 for books not worth a dime. The walls of the traditional secondhand business had been breached.

---

[5] My operations were disrupted when my daughter Meghan, eighteen at the time, decided she wanted to spend the summer as a waitress at a local restaurant instead of at the bookstore. She was such a hard worker and so efficient she was irreplaceable, but she had worked for me for six years and wanted a change of scenery. After a summer of grubbing for tips, though, she discovered that working for the old man wasn't so bad after all. She returned to the bookstore the next summer—the prodigal daughter.

To add insult to injury, once the internet operations had the booksellers in their thrall, Amazon and eBay systematically raised their fees, squeezing ever more blood out of these hapless turnips. The pressure was relentless. On the one hand, you had a virtual store—the internet, always open, with a nearly infinite selection of books at the lowest possible prices. On the other, you had a secondhand store with odd hours, an eccentric owner, a minuscule selection (relatively speaking), and higher prices. Not a real tough choice for the consumer.

By 2000 I knew the impact of the internet on the business was going to be permanent. Book searches, a big part of my business, were obsolete. Search companies that had done over $1 million a year in business went belly up in a matter of months. eBay still produced sales, but nothing like the early years. Sales through the other online services became so mediocre I stopped using them entirely. I did well at the store during the summer, but the winters were brutal. Throughout the country, being in the secondhand book business was like being in a war zone, with everyone around you either dead or dying. It never totally collapsed, just became a low-margin, competitive grind, like selling groceries but without the free steaks.

To add to Stillwater's woes, between 1997 and 2000 the Book Town started to unravel. Traffic from dealers and collectors slowed down. We still put on the book fair, but it got harder to sign up dealers. People came to Stillwater to see the Book Town, especially in the summer, but in a severe blow, Paul Kisselburg and Mark Douglas had to close the Stillwater Book Center in 1998 because the landlord would not renew their lease, so the Book Town lost thirty dealers in one fell swoop.

Paul describes the changes he noticed at the Book Center from his perspective: "The Book Center was open for three

St. Croix Antiquarian Books in 2017.

years. You and Tom had it for slightly more than one year. We noticed a significant drop in dealer traffic after the first year. The public bought more the second year to fill the gap. They did not during the third year. Dealers were no longer traveling to buy books, but something was also affecting the general public. Much of the decline in business later was caused by the internet, but I believe something else was going on before this. Not sure what, but there were fewer people buying books at the Center during the third year even though the quality of the books therein was at its highest."

Late in 1999 Tom told me he wanted to sell me his share of the building at 232 South Main and buy a bigger building: the old Reed Drug store down the block, roughly three times the size of 232. He stocked this with 150,000 books and turned it into a beautiful bookstore that he called Loome Antiquarian Books. It was one of the largest secondhand bookstores in the Midwest the day it opened. With Tom's new store, Stillwater still had half a million books within a four-block area, and that allowed us to keep pushing the book town idea for a few more years.

The sale of Tom's half of 232 to me was completed in January 2000. So, after ten years in Stillwater, I was the sole owner of the building on Main Street. After Tom took out his eighty thousand books and his half of the bookcases, St. Croix Books looked pretty empty, so over the next two years I built my stock up to thirty-five thousand books. I rearranged things so there were ten-foot-high bookcases around the perimeter of the front room and smaller, five-foot-tall cases along a center aisle; the back room had a similar arrangement. It was an impressive-looking store, with the wood floor Tom and I put in, the rare book room, and the center aisle flanked with books.

Despite the money I put into it, the physical condition of 232 South Main was a constant problem. Soon after my twelve-year-old son Colin started working there, he put a message on my desk that read:

> Dear Pop.
>
> If you are reading this then I'm already dead. I died in the back room from hypothermia because you insist on keeping it the temperature of a meat locker. I am forwarding a copy of this letter to the child abuse department and I hope they lock you away for a long time, you cruel, cruel man. I can only hope that no one else has to live through the horrible experience I did. Goodbye.
>
> Colin
>
> P.S. Would it be too much trouble to get some hot water in the bathroom?

By 2000 the domination of the business by the machines was complete. The once proud used bookseller became a soulless drone working for Amazon, eBay, and ABE. On the margins, things held steady into the early 2000s. It took some people, especially older people, time to find the internet, and some die-hard book people held out, Luddites at least for a while. Used booksellers, of course, were not alone. Video stores, music stores, antique stores, newspapers, taxi drivers, and new book dealers all felt the effects of the internet, but it is an underappreciated fact how extreme the effect was on the secondhand book trade.

As the internet's tentacles spread, people would come in and say, "There's nothing like an old bookstore. I just love the smell." Or "I'll never buy a book on Amazon. I want to see what I'm getting." Or "I'll never get a Kindle. I like real books." Noble sentiments, but abandoned if the book was online for a dollar less or you could download a digital copy in an instant. Movements like Buy Local and Save Our Secondhand Bookstore sprang up whenever a store was going under and might create an initial rush, but before long the charity buys died out and people went back to buying books on Amazon. In the end, nothing trumps price and convenience. If a store—any store—can't stand on its own two feet and survive in the world it lives in, it will fail, no matter how many well-wishers would like a different outcome.

A recent example is the Strand Book Store in New York City, one of the original, and last remaining, stores on the famous Book Row mentioned in chapter 10. In October 2020, its owner appealed to book lovers to #SaveTheStrand, and they responded by ordering twenty-five thousand books online. This is a testament to the nostalgic feelings people have about old bookstores, but like so many of these campaigns it will prove to be a futile gesture.

By 2000 I had two kids in college and had spent most of the money I made in the golden years supporting my family, buying more books, and buying the store from Tom, so despite the success of the past several years, I still barely had two nickels to rub together. The Book Center had closed, Tom had left St. Croix Books, and the Book Town was on life support. I would last until 2017, so I had to live with the internet monster for another seventeen years. (Fortunately for you, dear reader, the next seventeen years will go a lot faster than the first eighteen.[6]) I needed a new idea, and it couldn't be just another way to sell used books, since everything that could be tried was being tried in that desperate business.

---

[6] I hired Mike Frain around 1999, and he worked for me for nearly twenty years. Mike was a retired postal executive, not exactly a spring chicken when I took him on, but he was a great employee. He was a scholar and a collector. Besides books, he collected and sold toys, medieval weapons, old guns, and whatever else caught his fancy. He once lent me a full suit of medieval armor to display in the store. Besides that, he was an accomplished musician whose band played at St. Croix Books whenever we had a party or celebration. Mike was a true Renaissance man.

17. Survival Tactics

*Someone has to do something. It's just
incredibly pathetic it has to be us.*
JERRY GARCIA, *The Grateful Dead*

MY BEST IDEA came at the end of 2004, when I bought three folders of hand-painted architectural plans and prints that a Rochester architect had taken from a journal called the *American Architect and Building News* (*AABN*). The pictures included the names and locations of the buildings depicted and were beautifully colored. Perhaps, I thought, the buildings' current owners—if the buildings still existed—might be interested in them. I looked up one, a church in Illinois, found out it was still there, and contacted the church's pastor. He was quite excited; he didn't know a plan of his church even existed. I contacted other churches, schools, and businesses and they were also interested in these unique pictures.

Some background on these architectural plans, produced when the field of architecture was in its infancy. Before 1865 or so architecture wasn't even considered a profession—the first school was opened in 1868 at the Massachusetts Institute of Technology. Architecture's rise was fueled by the Gilded Age, when the so-called robber barons (Andrew Carnegie, Cornelius Vanderbilt, John D. Rockefeller, and J.P. Morgan) financed the construction of thousands of colleges, hospitals, museums, academies, schools, opera houses, and public libraries. The *AABN*, the first weekly journal for professional architects, was published between 1876 and 1909 and featured plans of houses and buildings either scheduled to be built or under construction. An 1875 issue, for instance, might have plans of St. Matthew's Church in Springfield, Illinois, or the Berkshire Hotel in New York City.

The *AABN* also featured architectural plans of places like P. T. Barnum's house in Bridgeport, Connecticut; Theodore Roosevelt's house on Long Island, New York; and Alexander Graham Bell's house in Baddeck, Nova Scotia. The plans could run for several pages, with each page showing a detailed view of a building or its interior.

There was a popular interest in the houses architects designed for the wealthy and powerful—not unlike the current "lifestyles of the rich and famous" TV shows, where viewers get to peek in at the garages and toilets of wealthy housewives and rap stars—and the public avidly followed their careers.

One of the more notorious was Stanford White, a founding partner of the architectural firm McKim, Mead, and White in New York City, the leading architectural design company in the country at the time. White designed, among other buildings, Madison Square Garden, the Washington Square Arch, and mansions for the Vanderbilts and the Astors. He began as an assistant to Henry Hobson Richardson,[1] widely considered the greatest architect of the time, and worked for him for six years before joining up with McKim and Mead.

---

[1] Despite being one of the most highly regarded—and highly paid—architects of the era, Richardson was deeply in debt when he died in 1886 at the age of forty-seven of Bright's disease. His wife and six children were left penniless, and Mrs. Richardson routinely begged the three architects who took over her husband's business for money to pay the coal bills and to buy shoes for the little Richardson children. Richardson is known for the style named for him, Richardsonian Romanesque, which he employed in building libraries, city halls, and courthouses.

Stanford White was a tall, flamboyant man with red hair and a red mustache who impressed others as witty, kind, and generous. The newspapers described him as "masterful," "intense," "burly yet boyish." His architectural work made him wealthy, and he spent lavishly on rare artwork and antiquities. His family lived on a large estate called Box Hill on Long Island and White maintained a multistory apartment with a rear entrance on Twenty-Fourth Street in Manhattan.

As the newspapers tell it, White gave the appearance of being happily married to his wife, Bessie, who minded Box Hill and the children while White worked in the city. Rumors, though, swirled that White carried on numerous affairs and had, in his apartment, a red velvet swing with ivy-twined ropes that hung from the ceiling. A movie about White called *The Girl in the Red Velvet Swing* was released in 1955 and was going to star Marilyn Monroe, but she refused to do the film because she thought it was too violent and risqué. (Marilyn had standards.) This sordid affair was also recently chronicled in a book called *The Girl on the Velvet Swing: Sex, Murder, and Madness at the Dawn of the Twentieth Century* by Simon Baatz.

One of White's affairs had disastrous consequences. On June 25, 1906, he attended the premiere of a play called *Mam'zelle Champagne* at Madison Square Garden. During the show's final song, "I Could Love a Million Girls," a man named Henry Thaw, whose wife had had an affair with White, walked up to him and said, "You've ruined my wife!" and then shot him three times, twice in the face and once in the shoulder. White died instantly.

After the murder, there followed what was described as the trial of the century, aided by sensationalized news coverage in the tabloids owned by William Randolph Hearst. Reporters seized on any person, place, or event, no matter how thinly it was connected to White's murder, in this, the heyday of tabloid journalism. Hard-boiled male reporters were matched by their sympathetic female counterparts, called the "sob sisters" and the "pity patrol."

The *AABN* also featured plans and photos of major building projects. One of the most extensive was the 1893 Chicago World's Fair, called the Columbian Exposition in honor of Christopher Columbus. Chicago architects Daniel Burnham and John Root invited the top architects in the United States to design the buildings for the fair, and luminaries like Peabody and Stearns; McKim, Mead, and White; A. Page Brown; and Adler and Sullivan accepted. The plans for the exposition were laid out by Burnham and Root and their third partner, Charles B. Atwood, in the then popular Beaux Arts style. The walkways and gardens were designed by landscape architect Frederick Law Olmsted. When the facades of the fair's buildings were built they were covered in white stucco, causing the exposition to be nicknamed "the White City."

Throughout 1893 and 1894 the *AABN* featured photographs and plans of the buildings designed for a fair that covered 690 acres, had two hundred new (but temporary) buildings of neoclassical design, and represented forty-six countries. The fair also featured carnival rides, among them the original Ferris wheel built by George Washington Gale Ferris Jr., which was 264 feet high and had thirty-six cars, each of which could accommodate forty people. More than twenty-seven million people attended the exposition during its six-month run. For those who like some intrigue with their architectural history, Erik Larson has an interesting treatment of the Columbian Exposition in his 2003 book *The Devil in the White City*, in which he juxtaposes the fair with the activities of Dr. Henry Howard Holmes, the first documented American serial killer.

When I bought the folders, I also bought several bound volumes of the *AABN* with hundreds of uncolored drawings. I had Carla Holmquist, an artist who worked for me, color some of these, and her work was as good as or better than the originals. Based on the interest in the pictures and Carla's ability to color more, I started a new business that we called St. Croix Architecture and over four years built up a stock of a few thousand of these hand-colored pictures and original photographs.

Besides the plans for the international buildings, there were plans for buildings built by the various states, like California and Rhode Island, that we sold to state historical societies, most of which had never seen the pictures before. By rescuing these plans and creating a market for them, we influenced the study of architecture as much as any academic treatise. Even now, if you Google one of the architects mentioned here you will find examples of the plans we produced.[2]

In 2009 I hosted an exhibit called *Victorian Architecture* covered in both the St. Paul and Minneapolis papers. According to *St. Paul Pioneer Press* reporter Mary Divine:

> Gary Goodman claims to have collected the world's most extensive set of original, hand-colored 19th century architectural plans and prints. He got his start in architectural drawings after he bought the private collection of a Rochester architect, a collection that he (the architect) had built over more than fifty years. Goodman then scoured eBay and bookstores for more drawings. He estimates that he has more than 2500 hand-colored plates,

---

[2] My youngest child, Steven, turned twelve and started working at the store at the end of 2007. Even then, he knew more about computers and the internet than I did, and I had worked with them since 1995. Like my other kids, he was a great worker but had, sadly, been corrupted by his sister and brothers and complained about the cold and lack of hot water in the bathroom. Come on, people. They call it work for a reason.

original gelatines, lithographs and photogravures in his collection. It includes churches, colleges, city halls, post offices, lighthouses, and steam ships. Customers have purchased architectural drawings and plans because they have a connection to the place or "just because they like the way they look," he said. "They are all one-of-a-kind . . . I've sold a lot to historical societies, and I've sold a lot to people who actually live in the houses." Many customers are architects themselves who are interested in the works of Cass Gilbert, H. H. Richardson, Daniel Burnham and John Root, Goodman said.

By 2009 I did as much business through St. Croix Architecture as I did through St. Croix Books. Colin, eighteen by this time, created a website for the business, and from this we sold pictures to places like Harvard and Princeton and just about every state historical society in the country. They told me how valuable the website was to them—some teachers even used it for their classes—and in 2010 I was invited to display and discuss these pictures at the Society of Architectural Historians.

From a business standpoint, the great thing about the architectural plans was that there was no competition. If I put a plan of a house or other building on eBay, it was the only one available, but they did have a limited market. If you sold one to the pastor of a church in Illinois, you might be able to sell another one to a member of the congregation, but that would be it. It was a constant battle to come up with new items.

Meanwhile, the book business in Stillwater and elsewhere kept deteriorating. A tax dispute with the city led Tom to close Loome Antiquarian Booksellers in 2007. Like everybody else, Tom was losing business to the internet, but he used the controversy to complain about the high property taxes in Still-water. As he put it in an October 2007 letter to the editor of the *Stillwater Gazette*:

> What's the solution? I frankly don't know, but it's been made brutally clear that it's not a matter of concern to the powers that be. Washington County's tax bureau-crats have let us know that the fate of downtown Still-water is not their concern. Their job is to do the numbers and damn the consequences. This is probably as good a time as ever to announce that Loome Antiquarian Booksellers (201 S. Main, southeast corner of Chestnut and Main) will close its doors at the end of 2007. After 17 years of selling books in our downtown stores, it is the tax man who has finally driven us to ground. Count therefore on one more large empty building in down-town Stillwater.

The next year, 2008, Tom decided to get out of the book busi-ness altogether and sold his main operation, Loome Theologi-cal Booksellers, to two of his employees. In a retirement tribute to Tom, I remarked that he was one of the few booksellers I knew who had made it out of the business alive. Tom died ten years later, in 2018, at the age of eighty-three. He was a great partner and friend—truly a force in the history of bookselling in Minnesota.

Also in 2008 was the Great Recession, and secondhand bookstores were dropping like flies. Most of the Chicago book-stores Paul Kisselburg and I had gone to went out of business, and many of the Twin Cities bookstores were either dead or dy-ing. In May 2010 we celebrated the twentieth anniversary of St. Croix Books. Mary Ann Grossmann's article in the *St. Paul Pio-neer Press* that month reflected the changes to the book business:

"I wonder how many years are left for stores that sell used books," Gary Goodman muses. "We face a difficult future." Still, this veteran bookseller is celebrating 20 years in a business that has seen 70 percent of the nation's brick and mortar rare and used bookstores close in the last six years. "Selling on the internet eventually produced a race to the bottom," says Goodman, who no longer sells books online. "Books that used to sell for $25 to $30, the lifeblood of used bookstores, can be found on the internet for a dollar. It's like the Wild West." Used bookstores also struggle with new printing technology that allows customers to buy an inexpensive print-on-demand book that might have cost $300 at a used bookstore. Or the customer can find an out-of-print book in an e-book format.

Over the next few years I sold other things to make up for the decline in book sales. I put in globes. I sold T-shirts based on books. I sold coffee and tea, again with a book theme.[3] For old-line bookstores things became increasingly dire. Some on the verge of closing tried that last gasp of the dying business —the GoFundMe campaign. These appealed to cat ladies, people who wore T-shirts that said "So Many Books, So Little Time," and others who loved old bookstores but rarely bought any books. These desperate appeals might help the stores survive for a few months, but in the end they still closed their doors.

I tried other things as well. A local theater group asked if they could put on plays at the store to raise money to buy a

---

[3] A cheerful addition to our staff around this time was my niece Hillary King, who helped design packaging and promotional materials for those ventures.

building for a permanent space, so I had Roger Hilde, who worked for me at the time, build a stage and put some bookcases on wheels so they could be moved when necessary. We called this the Goodman Theater, and, for two years, the theater group staged a play at the store nearly every month. Getting the store ready and the other things involved were a lot of work and not all that profitable, but if nothing else it brought some much-needed culture to downtown Stillwater.

In another venture, St. Croix Books published *The Secret History of Golf in Scotland,* mostly written by Mark Ziegler under the pseudonym Duncan MacPherson. I was listed as a coauthor. We used the old "found manuscript" device to describe how we came upon the book: "The author of this book, Duncan MacPherson, walked—unannounced—into St. Croix Antiquarian Booksellers on a cold day in January 2004. He carried a hand-written, dog-eared stack of papers he called *The Secret History of Golf in Scotland* in a brown package wrapped in twine." It's about a golf tournament in a small town in Scotland in 1534. The townspeople wager a lot of money on the participants; Lord Galbraith, the governor of the town, hires a ringer from Edinburgh to come and play to try and fix the outcome. There's a murder and several very odd characters, including a goat girl. Mark, citing his artistic sensibilities, insisted on including some salty and inappropriate scenes in the book, over my strong objections. It was published in a limited edition, and sales were, indeed, limited.

By the time St. Croix Books reached its twenty-fifth anniversary in 2015, I was ready to quit. After thirty-three years of fighting the good fight, I announced that I wanted to sell my building. In July of that year, Mary Divine from the *St. Paul Pioneer Press,* who so generously covered our efforts over the years, covered this as well:

"It's a real dying kind of thing—a used bookstore like this," Goodman said. "It's unfortunate, because there's so much here that you would never get a chance to see if you're just going online, or if you're just looking for a specific thing." He marveled for a moment about the writings of former president James Madison, a body of work Goodman said took the better part of a lifetime to compile. "Or, *The History of the Anglo-Saxons,*" he said. "You know, that guy probably spent 20 years on those books, putting them together and writing it. You just don't get a chance to see that kind of human effort if you start to believe that everything is instantaneous."

I finally found a buyer for the building in 2017 and announced the closing with what I called the Last Party. All the local newspapers and TV stations covered this. I'll let some of the articles that came out describe how it all ended:

Once the crown jewel of Stillwater's book scene, St. Croix Antiquarian Booksellers has announced that it will close after 27 years in business on Main Street. The store specializes in used, antique and out-of-print books, as well as antique maps and prints. The store was first opened in 1990 by Gary Goodman, Jim Cummings and Tom Loome. After Cummings left the business, Goodman and Loome opened a Book Center across the street that included books from 30 dealers from across the nation. Goodman estimated that at one point there were 500,000 books within a four-block radius. This haven for book lovers attracted national and even international attention, gaining Book Town status from Richard Booth, the "king" of the Welsh book town Hay-on-Wye. (Jackie Bussjaeger, Press Publications, March 17, 2017)

Back when Gary Goodman got into the used book business, he admits, he knew nothing about running a used bookstore. At the time, he was seeking respite from his work as a counselor on a psychiatric unit. Now, 27 years after opening St. Croix Antiquarian Booksellers on Main Street in Stillwater, Goodman is once again seeking a change: retirement. The longtime used and rare bookstore is closing at the end of July. "It helped me put six kids through college," he said on a recent morning, as customers browsed the aisles looking for bargains. "But it's a rough business, especially in this day and age." (James Walsh, *Star Tribune,* March 19, 2017)

"It will be sad to see it go, but I'm ready," said Goodman, who lives in Stillwater. "I'm not getting any younger. I have six kids, but none are foolish enough to get into the used book business." Longtime employee Carla Holmquist will buy part of Goodman's business: a rare collection of original hand-colored 19th century architectural drawings from around the world. "I want to thank our customers from Stillwater and around the world—Russia, India, Tibet, Australia, Singapore, you name it—who have supported us for the past 27 years," Goodman said. "I am proud to have been the owner of what is widely regarded as one of the last great used bookstores in the Midwest." (Mary Divine, *St. Paul Pioneer Press,* March 18, 2017)

But just because I sold the building didn't mean I was safely out of the book business. I still had forty thousand books. Why not just sell the building and the books together, you might ask—surely someone would want to buy such a well-known bookstore? And a couple of people did, but only on a pay-as-you-go basis. These never seemed to work. People who took over existing stores usually sold all the decent books in a year or two and then would go belly up. (Remember Mike, the guy who bought my Arcade Street store? He lasted a year and a half, about as long as it took him to sell the books he had bought from me.) My goal was to get out of the book business alive—not, as we have seen, always easy to do—so I decided to sell the books myself: from March to September 2017 I offered them for sale at increasing discounts, and then, at the end, another bookseller came in and offered me a dollar apiece for the thirteen thousand that were left, which I gladly took.

Looking back, I have complained about the building at 232 throughout this story—it leaked, it was cold, it didn't have hot water—but the store and its success have been a source of great pride. I remember all the people who would come in over the years and tell me how it was a dream of theirs to own a bookstore. Sometimes I would think, "If you only knew." But I recognize what a gift it has been to be in this chaotic and fascinating business.

And, sure, buying that Arcade Street store and those four thousand bad books was a rash decision. I was lucky to survive a year, much less until I moved to Stillwater. Only stubbornness, and a genuine love of books, kept me going. A sensible person would have told you that a secondhand bookstore on that block in East St. Paul couldn't survive, but then again a sensible person probably wouldn't have gotten into the used book business in the first place.

Epilogue

Just like one of us, the monkey
folds its arms in the autumn wind.
BASHO

THE SUMMER after I sold my building, Nolan talked me into going to the Midwest Bookhunters book fair at the Minnesota State Fairgrounds. It was a hot June day, the temperature in the nineties, and the Progress Center, where the fair was being held, wasn't air-conditioned, so big fans blew on the sweaty, sparse crowd in attendance. This fair was once hard to get into, but now anyone with a few boxes of scruffy books could get a booth, and even then it was only half full. Most of the exhibitors were at least sixty years old and the customers, if anything, were older. As we walked through the fair, I ran into some old bookseller friends and asked how things were going.

As usual, talk turned to the dismal state of the book business. A couple wondered if the business would ever get back to the way it used to be. "Things go in cycles," one observed. "They're slow now, but that's part of the process. People like real books and they love old bookstores, so it's just a matter of time before it all turns around." His partner, less optimistic, said, "The only way it will come back is with the collapse of Western civilization. No more internet. No more e-machines. People living in caves. The book business is dead, and I'm just hoping to hang on until I can collect my Social Security."

That booksellers now survive only on the thin gruel doled out by their internet masters is borne out by a 2019 documentary called *The Booksellers,* which follows some book dealers the director, D. W. Young, meets at the New York International Antiquarian Book Fair. Through interviews and a history of the formerly great New York book scene, the film tries to generate hope for the bookstores still in existence. It covers the usual ground: how fascinating used books are, how everybody loves old bookstores, and how maybe, just maybe, the internet is a passing fad. The problem is, most of the booksellers in the movie are really old and can't stop grousing about how the internet ruined their businesses. In the March 2020 issue of the *New Yorker,* Anthony Lane says of this documentary, "It's a ghost story, brooded over by the rustling wraiths of bookstores dead and gone."

This, too, has been a ghost story. A story about some of the last people in the traditional secondhand book business. My contribution has been the Arcade Street store, Stillwater, and the Book Town tales, but the story is also told through other people and places: criminals like John Jenkins and Stephen Blumberg, characters like Melvin McCosh and Larry McMurtry, book towns like Archer City and Hay-on-Wye. On the fringes the quoters, book scouts, and collectors rummaged around in the basement of the human mind and brought things to light that otherwise would have been lost. If the story has a villain, it is the internet. When the internet was small, booksellers fed it all their secrets. When it got big, it ate them up. This once human business is now dominated by the machines that have made it impossible for traditional secondhand stores to survive.

The logic and economics of this are inescapable. As much as some might want old bookstores to still be around, and swashbuckling booksellers to be out hunting books, they have lost the reason for their existence. They are no longer needed to find, or provide, secondhand or out-of-print books. The life depicted here, that of traveling booksellers and the traditional secondhand bookstore, is over. Soon, the only bookstores left worthy of the name will be the independent stores that sell new books—businesses the internet hasn't figured out how to replace. They deserve your support. Get off the internet and out of the house. Buy a real book.

The larger question is if even the physical book can survive, and here there might be some reason for optimism. One is reminded of a talk Isaac Asimov, the great science fiction writer, gave called "The End of the Book" at the American Booksellers Convention in 1989. A participant at the convention described Asimov's talk as follows:

> He offered a futurist's argument on why the book could not possibly survive. He concluded his elegy for the book with an impassioned and hopeful description of something that might endure and outlast the book. He described an object that would be portable; it would need no power source but light, natural or artificial; would last for years if cared for, could easily be shared with others; could be mass-produced and sold cheaply. He then reached into the back pocket of his faded jeans and pulled out a dog-eared paperback book. He held it up and told us we were looking at the endpoint of technology, an invention that could never be improved upon, and that would never be replaced.

As long as new books are printed and become used, secondhand, and rare books, someone is going to sell them. It is the process and the people that have changed. What I have tried to do here, in my limited way, is to present a picture of what the odd and glorious secondhand book business was like before the internet took over. And, okay, I'm sorry, I know I'm not the last bookseller, but if you mean a certain kind of bookseller, I'm probably pretty close.

APPENDIX *Travel Journal*

I include this unedited journal because it gives an idea of what life on the road looking for books and traveling from place to place was like for booksellers. This was the lifeblood of the business, but it could be stressful and frustrating. There were a lot of dark holes, red herrings, and dead ends, but the rare great finds made it all worth it.

11/04/93. Arrived Hartford Tues. Two stores yesterday— The Book Exchange ($93) in Plainville, which was pretty poor, and the Bibliolatree in East Hampton. Spent all afternoon at the latter. Quite good, but everything disorganized. Spent $644—good travel and exploration—high on the obvious things, but worth returning to. The Picasso book I bought there turned out to be less of a buy than I thought.

11/05/93. Spent this entire day in New Haven, first at Coventry Books, which is primarily academic remainders. Got many good titles for $1.98 and some other good things—the guys that runs the store has another one in Cambridge near Harvard that does much better than this one, which is near Yale. He says the Yale students don't buy books. They only care about drugs and chasing tail. Spent $425 there.

Went to Arethusa Books again and found some good things, including a set of Rickett's *Wildflowers* for $600. Spent $1000 total. Can tell he doesn't turn over much and his prices seem to be going up. Still, a worthwhile stop.

Wound up at Whitlock's, which is run by an older man who is looking at his final years in the book business. Quite gentlemanly, but his stock was obviously worn out. Found some good history and biography. You can tell this business is a younger man's game—you need a certain amount of hustle to keep the momentum. Anyway, left New Haven and drove nearly to Wilmington DE through New York City, which wasn't as difficult as I'd thought it would be.

11/06/93. Made my way to Newark DE and got to C. W. Mortenson's at about noon. Spent the entire day in this fellow's remodeled horse barn. He has some great things, especially Alaskan and travel, and I haven't even looked at the books in the house yet. He's quite elderly and is interested in selling all the books but I'm not sure what he'd want for them. He's quite interesting—a chemist and a lawyer who loves books. Those books in the barn haven't been looked at in years.

Had to empty my car to fit those books in so wound up rushing to a motel, wrapping the books, and taking them to Roadway. Return to Mortenson's in the AM.

11/07/93. Spent yesterday at Mortenson's wrapping up my dealings with him. Wound up with about 450 books, for which I paid $2350—some very good things and some stock, but I think I paid him a fair price. Spent until 11:00 PM wrapping the books, which I left at the Tally Ho Motel for Roadway to pick up. He did not want me to look at the books upstairs but invited me back some other time. I will have to do it in the spring because I'm afraid he'll die soon.[1]

11/08/93. Today I went to Cranberry Books in Cranbury NJ—it is a good stop—cheap books and some things not picked. Spent $168. Then went to Book Garden in Cream Ridge, NJ, which was very good. Cheap books and many sleepers. Spent $365 for 4 boxes. Took a wrong turn so now am in Brielle, NJ. Will spend the night and go to Escargot Books tomorrow.

11/09/93. Two stops today—did very well at Escargot Books. Also a bookstore nearby—Read It Again Books that the fellow at Escargot said was very good, but it is closed on Monday. Went to a store in Madison NJ that didn't have much, but the books were cheap.

11/10/93. Went to A. Lucas Books in Fairfield, CT before heading to the airport. I'd been there before but had forgotten. This is a retired mail carrier—78 years old—who has horrendously overpriced books that he'll sell for 3 and 5 dollars if you press him. Spent $306.

01/12/94. Arrived in Newark yesterday and drove into New York City today. Wet, heavy snow. Drove along Madison Ave.

---

[1] I did return to Mortenson's a couple of months later and bought all his books—probably five thousand or so. I hired a guy from Stillwater to pack the books for me while I traveled around the East buying books. When I got back, I found out he just stuffed the books into huge boxes and tossed them out of the second story of the horse barn. Old man Mortenson had to stop him. What a disaster. After flying him out there and paying his expenses, I ended up packing most of the books myself.

to the Upper East Side. People everywhere, pushing carts, riding bikes in the snow right through the traffic. Still, things move along quite well. Went to Barbara Spector's—the lady has 5,000 books, but I misread the situation. She was not a collector, as she led me to believe, but the owner of an antique shop whose husband had a weakness for cheap books.

The books were bad, for the most part, and would have been very hard to move in any event. Two thousand or so were in a "studio" up two long flights of stairs and the others were in her store or apartment. She told me over the phone that she wanted $30,000 for the books. When I got there and told her I didn't want them, she said, "How about $2000?"

When I still said no, she said I could just have them. I told her they just weren't salable books, at which point she started sobbing and said she had to get them out of the apartment by the end of the month because she and her husband had been evicted. I said if I was from New York I'd try to help her but since I was from Minnesota there was nothing I could do. The apartment was ungodly hot and had all kinds of cats wandering around who weren't particular about where they went to the bathroom. I felt sorry for her but was glad to get out of there.

01/13/94. Spent the day in Worcester—went to three stores and spent about $765. Two—Ben Franklin and a place at 940 Main—were pretty good. The other, called A Likely Story, was poor.

01/14/94. Today got to Miriam Redlo's in Framingham at 11:00 AM and spent until 4 PM buying books. Last time I was there was the summer of 1992, even though it doesn't seem nearly that long. Spent $1172 for eight boxes of pretty good books. She is quite interesting: lives with her son Eric, who is a goofball. He spent nearly ten thousand dollars buying copies of Madonna's book, *Sex,* at $50 a copy and now his mother is stuck trying to unload them. Miriam has a Ph.D. in Psychology, retired, I like her quite a bit. She is somewhat weary of the book business but, like many, compulsively persists. Later, I stopped at Bearly Read Books, which is quite bad. I did not buy a book. Shipped fourteen boxes this evening.

01/15/94. The weather took its toll on this trip today because my rental car wouldn't start. I wound up waiting until 3:30 PM for the car company to bring another car from Boston. Made it to Howard Feldstein's by 4:30 but was not able to look at much. Looks like a pretty good store and will go back tomorrow.

03/06/98. Have been to Chicago, Milwaukee, and Great Britain in the past two months. Chicago and Milwaukee are pretty much the same. Did very well in England. Spent about $20,000 (cash) on 38 boxes of books. Went with Paul Kisselburg this time, so the logistics were much better.

04/24/98. On a trip to Missouri and Arkansas with Ben so he can practice golf. We drove to within fifty miles of Kansas City the first day and then down to Springfield today.

04/25/98. Stores on this trip:

- ABC Books. Spent $240 here but it is a pretty dismal store. Primarily religious with a lot of ex-library. Owner said she is putting a lot of books online so not everything she had was out.

– Half-Price Books. Not part of the chain. Mostly paperbacks but also hardcovers in good condition. Got lucky and bought a few gun books that just came in. Spent $327.

– Shirley's. Right down the block. Gave me 40% off because she said she's closing and just going to list on the internet. Miserable place.

– Hooked on Books. Pretty decent. In a hurry because they were about to close. Spent $122.

05/08/98 to 07/04/98. Went to Vancouver and Great Britain with Paul. Went to Alaska. The Vancouver trip was for four days and I bought 25 boxes. The Britain trip wasn't as productive as in the past—23 boxes—because we stopped in Amsterdam. You can't buy books there.

Bought some Arctic and Antarctic books shortly after I got back from Alaska from an elderly man who had spent his working life as a missionary in Japan. Very good books. Included some of the classics by Ernest Shackleton, Robert Peary, and Robert Scott. Even more interesting were his stories of working, in the 1950s, with the Ainu tribe who lived on the northern island of Hokkaido in Japan. The Ainu were an indigenous Japanese tribe whose last full-blooded member died in 1973. They were known as the "Hairy Ainu" because the men did not shave or cut their hair. They had a reverence for the bears they hunted for food and clothing and he sold me two beautiful wooden carvings of bears they made. One was a large carving of a mother bear with two cubs and the other, smaller one, was of a bear with a salmon in its mouth. I sold the larger carving, but still have the smaller one.

08/13/98. Currently on a trip to New Hampshire. Tough first day in Portsmouth. Book Guild—spent $295—and went to Northwoods Books (horrible). All stores pretty bad until I got to Lee Burt in Laconia. She is an older woman with children's books and other stuff. Bought eight boxes for $1,250. 10 boxes total. Tomorrow will go to Kalonbooks—up Hwy 114—where I was four years ago.

08/14/98. Did very well at Kalonbooks. Spent $1,750 on about ten boxes. Went to Books by the Lake—spent $115 on one box. Not worth going back. Also went to the Book Farm, which was OK. Spent $295 on two boxes.

08/15/98. Just two stops today, but both were pretty good. First was Nelson's in Goshen. Spent $610 on four boxes plus $1300 on a set of Pooh firsts. Then drove to Keene and Eagle Books, where I spent $630 on five boxes.

Acknowledgments

I want to thank, first, the often-mentioned Paul Kisselburg. My friend reviewed early drafts of this book and has generously commented on every one. I expected him to disagree with my portrayal of him as a self-serving, obsessed bookseller—he isn't, really—but he didn't ask me to change a single word.

Thanks, too, to Dr. Pat Hicks of Augustana University in Sioux Falls, South Dakota, who not only teaches real writers in an MFA program there but has also written several books. He took the time to edit and comment on the manuscript. His help and encouragement have been invaluable.

Thanks to Erik Anderson, my editor at the University of Minnesota Press, whose own love of rare books made him see this book's potential. His sharp ear, clear mind, and kind heart have made this a much better book. A special thanks also goes to my copy editor, Madeleine Vasaly, for her eagle eye and insightful corrections.

Thanks to all my great employees over the years, including Mike Frain, Carla Holmquist, Hillary King, Dawn and Roger Hilde, Frank Hurley, Erin Peterson, Karen Brezinka, Tami Waters, Sara Trent, Peter King, Arthur Hudgins, and Judy Symalla.

Booksellers Ken Czech and Steve Anderson read a later draft and made helpful suggestions or corrected errors of fact, as did my brother, Ron Goodman, my friend Mark Ziegler, and my wife and grown children, to whom this book is dedicated. Any mistakes that remain are my own.

Bibliography

Agresta, Michael. "The Last Book Sale: An Era Ends for an Author, a Town, and a Culture." *The Atlantic*, August 22, 2012.

Anonymous. *The Private Papers of a Bankrupt Bookseller*. London: Jonathan Cape, 1936.

Basbanes, Nicholas. *A Gentle Madness: Bibliophiles, Bibliomanes, and the Eternal Passion for Books*. New York: Owl Books/Henry Holt, 1995.

Blanding, Michael. *The Map Thief*. New York: Avery, 2014.

Booth, Richard. *My Kingdom of Books*. Ceredigion, Wales: Y Lolfa, 1999.

Bryson, Bill. *The Mother Tongue: English and How It Got That Way*. New York: Morrow, 1990.

Bruno, Guido. *Adventures in American Bookshops*. Detroit: Douglas Bookshop, 1922.

Bussjaeger, Jackie. "St. Croix Antiquarian Booksellers Closes Its Doors." Press Publications, March 17, 2017.

Butts, William. *Absolutely, Mr. Sickles? Positively, Mr. Field!* Hollywood, Fla.: International Autograph Collectors Club & Dealers Alliance, 2001.

Buzbee, Lewis. *The Yellow-Lighted Bookshop*. St. Paul: Graywolf Press, 2006.

Bythell, Shaun. *Confessions of a Bookseller*. Boston: David R. Godine, 2020.

Bythell, Shaun. *The Diary of a Bookseller*. New York: Melville House, 2018.

Campbell, Jen. *The Bookshop Book*. London: Constable, 2014.

Curtis, Gregory. "Forgery, Texas Style." *Texas Monthly*, March 1989.

Daley, Jason. "Book of Lost Books Discovered in Danish Archive." *Smithsonian Magazine,* April 11, 2019.

Divine, Mary. "Stillwater Bookstore Owner Offers Glimpse of the Not-So-Faded Past." *St. Paul Pioneer Press,* December 2, 2009.

———. "Stillwater's St. Croix Antiquarian Booksellers for Sale." *St. Paul Pioneer Press,* July 26, 2015.

———. "Antiquarian Books Closing in July." *St. Paul Pioneer Press,* March 18, 2017.

———. "Thomas Loome, Who Sold Rare Books in Stillwater, Dies." *St. Paul Pioneer Press,* April 16, 2018.

Dunn, James Taylor. *The St. Croix.* New York: Holt, Rinehart & Winston, 1965.

Dunning, John. *Bookscout.* Minneapolis: Dinkytown Antiquarian Books, 1998.

Dylan, Bob. *Chronicles: Volume I.* New York: Simon & Schuster, 2004.

Ellman, Richard. *James Joyce.* New York: Oxford University Press, 1959.

Finnegan, William. "A Theft in the Library," *New Yorker,* October 17, 2005.

Fitzgerald, F. Scott. *The Crack-Up.* Harmondsworth: Penguin Books, 1965.

Grossmann, Mary Ann. " 'King Richard' Decrees Which Become Book Towns." *St. Paul Pioneer Press,* August 21, 1994.

———. "U Embraced Colorful Bookseller." *St. Paul Pioneer Press,* May 31, 2007.

———. "Used to It: St. Croix Antiquarian Celebrates 20 Years of Used Book Sales—Hanging on through Tough Times." *St. Paul Pioneer Press,* May 17, 2010.

Grove, Lee Edmonds. *Of Brooks and Books.* Minneapolis: University of Minnesota Press, 1945.

Harvey, Miles. *The Island of Lost Maps: A True Story of Cartographic Crime.* New York: Random House, 2000.

Hyman, Stanley Edgar. "Book Scout." *New Yorker,* November 8, 1952.

Innes, Brian. *Fakes and Forgeries: The True Crime Stories of History's Greatest Deceptions.* Pleasantville, New York: Reader's Digest, 2005.

Johnson, Alex. *Book Towns: Forty-Five Paradises of the Printed Word.* London: Frances Lincoln, 2018.

Johnston, Patricia. *Stillwater: Minnesota's Birthplace.* Afton, Minn.: Afton Historical Press, 1995.

Karr, Mary. *The Art of Memoir.* New York: Harper Collins, 2015.

Knight, Paul. "Will Archer City Survive Without Larry McMurtry's Bookstores?" *Texas Monthly,* January 21, 2013.

Kreitner, Richard. *Booked: A Traveler's Guide to Literary Locations around the World.* New York: Black Dog & Leventhal Publishers, 2019.

Lindsey, Robert. *A Gathering of Zion: A True Story of Money, Murder and Deceit.* New York: Simon and Schuster, 1988.

MacPherson, Duncan, and Gary Goodman. *The Secret History of Golf in Scotland.* Stillwater, Minn.: St. Croix Books, 2006.

McDade, Travis. *Thieves of Book Row: New York's Most Notorious Rare Book Ring and the Man Who Stopped It.* New York: Oxford University Press, 2013.

McMurtry, Larry. *Books: A Memoir.* New York: Simon and Schuster, 2009.

McMurtry, Larry. *In a Narrow Grave.* Austin: Encino Press, 1968.

McWilliams, James E. "Deal or No Deal: The Art of Scouting for Rare Books in the Age of the Internet." *Texas Observer,* August 11, 2006.

Mondlin, Marvin, and Roy Meador. *Book Row: An Anecdotal and Pictorial History of the Antiquarian Book Trade.* New York: Carroll & Graf Publishers, 2003.

Moreton, Cole. "Books: A Right Royal Pain." *Independent,* May 24, 1998.

Peterson, Brent. *Stillwater: Images of America.* Charleston: Arcadia Publishers, 2013.

Reback, Storms. "From the Poker Vaults: Austin Squatty." PokerNews. February 2009. https://www.pokernews.com/news/2009/02/poker-vaults-austin-squatty-1160-6191.htm.

Roberts, Sam. "Madeline Kripke, Doyenne of Dictionaries, Is Dead at 76." *New York Times,* April 30, 2020.

Romenesko, James. "Book Retailers Open New Chapter with Online Sales." *St. Paul Pioneer Press,* February 23, 1998.

Rosenbach, A. S. W. *Books and Bidders: The Adventures of a Bibliophile.* Boston: Little, Brown & Co., 1927.

Rydell, Anders. *The Book Thieves.* New York: Penguin Books, 2015.

Sillitoe, Linda, and Allen D. Roberts. *Salamander: The Story of the Mormon Forgery Murders.* Salt Lake City: Signature Books, 1988.

Trillin, Calvin. "Scouting Sleepers." *New Yorker,* June 14, 1976.
Walsh, James. "St. Croix Antiquarian Booksellers Closing in
    Downtown Stillwater." *Star Tribune,* March 19, 2017.
Wilson-Lee, Edward. *The Catalogue of Shipwrecked Books:
    Christopher Columbus, His Son, and the Quest to Build the
    World's Greatest Library.* New York: Scribner's, 2019.
Yuan, Karen, "A Crime Against Culture." *Atlantic,* December 19,
    2018.

GARY GOODMAN has been a used and rare book dealer for nearly forty years. He cofounded St. Croix Antiquarian Booksellers and the Stillwater Book Center in Stillwater, Minnesota, and started St. Croix Architecture, a business specializing in historic architectural prints. He is coauthor of the *Stillwater Booktown Times* and *The Secret History of Golf in Scotland*.